"I've known Jacqulyne Horbrook since she launch... teach and lead with heart and purpose. I honestly cannot think of a person more qualified to write this book. Her heart for God and for people is reflected on every page, challenging us and training us to steward our influence well, using it to serve God's mission. This book is not only a pragmatic guide for growing followers, but it is also a playbook for those who want to make a meaningful impact in the lives of those following them. *How to Be a Christian Influencer* is hands down the best book I've read on using social media as a Christian without losing yourself in the process."

David S. Winston, author and pastor of Living Word Christian Center

"Jacqulyne Horbrook has always set the tone with wisdom, practicality, and a heart for maximizing influence to glorify the kingdom. She was instrumental in helping me land my very first major brand deal as a Christian influencer, and for that I am forever grateful. I know this book is nothing short of amazing— not simply because Jackie wrote it, but because she lives what she teaches every single day!"

Whitney Moss, entrepreneur

"Jacqulyne Horbrook is a faithful guide for today's generation of Christian leaders trying to live out the Great Commission in a digital world. She has a unique voice for this moment, navigating the complex intersections of faith, culture, and digital influence with clarity and conviction. What makes her work stand out isn't just strategy; it's her deep belief that influence is a form of discipleship. She doesn't just teach how to build a platform; she models how to steward it with authenticity, courage, and integrity. Horbrook's story is not about chasing visibility; it's about choosing impact. Through personal sacrifice, strategic thinking, and deep spiritual grounding, she has cultivated a space where integrity meets innovation. *How to Be a Christian Influencer* isn't just a book—it's a blueprint for reclaiming purpose in a noisy world."

Terence Lester, founder of Love Beyond Walls and author of *I See You, When We Stand, All God's Children*, and *From Dropout to Doctorate*

"In a generation chasing clicks, Jacqulyne Horbrook calls us back to the Great Commission. This book is biblical, clear, and actionable. If you want to steward your platform with integrity, tell the truth in love, and point people to Jesus with every post, *How to Be a Christian Influencer* is the guide you need."

Albaner C. Eugene Jr., founder of ACEPRODUCTIONS

Jacqulyne Horbrook

HOW TO BE A
CHRISTIAN
INFLUENCER

Making Social Media
a Social Ministry

An imprint of InterVarsity Press
Downers Grove, Illinois

InterVarsity Press
P.O. Box 1400 | Downers Grove, IL 60515-1426
ivpress.com | email@ivpress.com

InterVarsity Press® is the publishing division of InterVarsity Christian Fellowship/USA®. For more information, visit intervarsity.org.

All Scripture quotations, unless otherwise indicated, are taken from The Holy Bible, New International Version®, NIV®. Copyright © 1973, 1978, 1984, 2011 by Biblica, Inc.™ Used by permission of Zondervan. All rights reserved worldwide. www.zondervan.com. The "NIV" and "New International Version" are trademarks registered in the United States Patent and Trademark Office by Biblica, Inc.™

While any stories in this book are true, some names and identifying information may have been changed to protect the privacy of individuals.

The publisher cannot verify the accuracy or functionality of website URLs used in this book beyond the date of publication.

Cover design: Amy Cerra
Interior design: Daniel van Loon

ISBN 978-1-5140-0992-5 (print) | ISBN 978-1-5140-0993-2 (digital)

Printed in the United States of America ∞

Library of Congress Cataloging-in-Publication Data
Names: Horbrook, Jacqulyne, 1984- author
Title: How to be a Christian influencer : making social media a social
   ministry / Jacqulyne Horbrook.
Description: Downers Grove, IL : IVP, [2026] | Includes bibliographical
   references.
Identifiers: LCCN 2025032034 (print) | LCCN 2025032035 (ebook) | ISBN
   9781514009925 paperback | ISBN 9781514009932 ebook
Subjects: LCSH: Social media–Religious aspects–Christianity | Internet in
   evangelistic work | Internet in church work | Internet personalities
Classification: LCC BV652.95 .H65 2026 (print) | LCC BV652.95 (ebook)
LC record available at https://lccn.loc.gov/2025032034
LC ebook record available at https://lccn.loc.gov/2025032035

31   30   29   28   27   26 | 13   12   11   10   9   8   7   6   5   4   3   2   1

To my beautiful daughters, Taylor and Maliah:

You are the reason I dared to step into my purpose. God has a way of using life's challenges to push us toward the extraordinary, and it was in my moments of uncertainty, facing the weight of providing for you, that I discovered my strength.

You both are my greatest blessings and my deepest motivation. Every step I've taken as an entrepreneur and influencer has been fueled by my love for you and my desire to create a life that reflects the power of faith, perseverance, and purpose.

It is so important to me to be an example of what it looks like to live for God and to trust in his power to create new and innovative things. My prayer is that as you grow, you will look back on what I have been able to accomplish and know that the same God who worked in my life is able to do even greater things in yours.

This book is for you—because without you, I may never have found the courage to pursue the calling God placed on my life. Thank you for being my light in the darkest moments and the reason I strive to be the best version of myself.

With all my love,

Mom

CONTENTS

THE CALL TO INFLUENCE

When people ask me about my call to influence, I always say it started long before I was even born. It began with my parents, Tanya and Michael Horbrook, who laid the foundation through their faith, integrity, and example. Their influence shaped the way I see the world, long before I ever realized I had a calling of my own.

I firmly believe that we inherit influence before we even learn how to wield it. Whether we realize it or not, we all start out under someone else's influence (good or bad), shaped by the prayers they prayed, the sacrifices they made, and the examples they set. My father in particular left an unforgettable mark. He wasn't just my dad—he was my first pastor, and through him, I learned what it meant to step boldly into my calling. His influence didn't come from big stages or bright lights. It started on the street corners of Chicago.

STREET MINISTRY AND THE DIGITAL AGE

My dad used to tell me a story about when he first became a minister. Back in the day, he'd grab his bullhorn and a stack of tracts and head out to the corner of 63rd Street and Ashland in

Englewood, Chicago, to preach the gospel. If you grew up in a traditional church setting, you probably already know what tracts are. But for those who didn't, tracts were small, pocket-sized brochures, often illustrated in a comic book style, designed to break down the message of Jesus in a way that was simple, creative, and impactful. Tracts were basically the Instagram posts of their time—short, bold, and meant to catch your attention.

It's funny to think how something so small could carry such a big message, but that was the whole point. These weren't just papers to pass out; they were tools of connection, conversation starters that could lead to transformation. And my dad knew how to use them. With his tracts in one hand and his bullhorn in the other, he was meeting people right where they were, creating a direct line between the message and those who needed to hear it.

THE METHOD HAS CHANGED, BUT THE MISSION REMAINS THE SAME— REACHING PEOPLE WHERE THEY ARE.

This wasn't some quiet, behind-the-pulpit kind of ministry. It was a street team ministry. The goal wasn't to fill a pew but to plant a seed. It was all about taking the church outside the four walls, meeting people in their everyday lives, and sharing the gospel in the most direct way possible.

And while it was effective, it didn't come without risks, some of which were life-threatening. One day, while my dad was preaching, a young man pulled a gun on him, attempting to rob him. Most of us would have dropped the bullhorn, handed over the wallet, and called it a day. But not my dad. Instead of freezing or backing down, he did something bold and maybe even a little crazy. He started singing. At the top of his lungs, he belted out, "One, one, one! One way to Jesus, baptized in Jesus' name!" Now, I'll be honest, my dad is not the greatest singer. But that didn't stop him. His voice got louder, his confidence grew, and he kept preaching with a gun pointed at him.

As he sang and preached, something shifted. The gunman changed his mind. Without a word, he turned and ran away, leaving my dad standing there with his bullhorn, his voice echoing through the streets of Chicago.

THE DIGITAL HIGHWAYS AND HEDGES

That story makes me think about the parallels between street team ministry and sharing the gospel on social media today. Sure, the tools are different—back then, it was bullhorns and tracts; now, it's hashtags and Instagram stories—but the concept is the same. Social media is like a digital street corner, giving us the opportunity to reach people who might never walk into a church. The potential to spread hope and truth to thousands, even millions, is right at our fingertips.

A staggering 72 percent of the public uses some form of social media.[1] That's not just a statistic but a wake-up call for believers who are serious about their calling to influence. On average, people spend two hours and thirty-one minutes per day on social media, with younger generations spending even more time. Studies project that social media users will grow to

5.85 billion by 2027, meaning that more than half the world's population will be actively engaging on these platforms.[2]

But with all that influence comes a responsibility. And history has shown us that influence can be a gift—or a weapon.

THE CORRUPTION OF INFLUENCE

Most people don't think of Lucifer as an influencer, but he was. Just not in a way that led to anything good.

Jealousy influenced Lucifer to rebel.

Lucifer influenced Eve to second-guess God's Word.

Eve influenced Adam to disobey, and just like that, sin went viral. One moment, they were living in paradise. The next, they were hiding, blaming each other, and figuring out life on the other side of Eden.

This is how influence works—it's shared. Just like a trending post, it moves from one person to the next, reshaping thoughts, decisions, and even destinies. A single moment of deception turned into humanity's most catastrophic repost. And the worst part? It couldn't be deleted.

Lucifer's mistake wasn't just rebellion. It was that he wanted more influence than he was given. Instead of using his influence to worship God, he wanted to be God.

Isaiah 14:13-14 records his exact words: "I will ascend to the heavens; I will raise my throne above the stars of God . . . I will make myself like the Most High."

Pride not only caused Lucifer's fall but also redefined his entire purpose. That same toxic cycle is still at work today. We've seen pastors fall when their platforms became more about their name than God's name. We've seen influencers who once stood for truth start compromising for clicks, views, and brand deals. We've seen leaders, celebrities, and everyday people allow their influence to shift from something pure to something self-serving.

Proverbs 16:18 makes it plain: "Pride goes before destruction, a haughty spirit before a fall."

That's why guarding our influence is so important. If the enemy can't stop us from having influence, he'll try to corrupt it.

Which brings us to a classic lesson in influence, straight from Saturday morning cartoons.

THE TOM AND JERRY DILEMMA

I remember watching *The Tom and Jerry Show* as a kid. Tom, the mischievous cat, would get stuck in a moral dilemma and suddenly, two tiny versions of himself would pop up on his shoulders. On one side, the good angel—halo shining, voice calm, telling him to walk away and make the right choice. And on the other? The bad angel, red with a pitchfork, hyping him up to do something reckless.

That, my friends, is influence in action. Every day, we have voices in our ears nudging us toward decisions—some wise, some disastrous.

In this world of social media, it is extremely easy to lose yourself and become enticed by the notoriety that comes with being an influencer. These days, it doesn't take much to become an influencer on social media. A nice website and a few catchy quotes can be enough for people to jump on the bandwagon without hesitation. But with the price of influence so low and the demand for it so high, we are often left to swim in a sea of saltwater, thirsty for anyone with relevant-sounding solutions. Our faith in God has waxed cold as our hope in humankind grows stronger with every well-captioned post. We are living in the days that Jesus spoke of in Matthew 24:5: "For many shall come in my name, saying, I am Christ; and shall deceive many" (KJV). Just look around. Every day we see more and more experts, gurus, and influencers come to the surface claiming to hold the keys to success, deceiving many who desire to be quenched.

RECLAIMING THE PURPOSE OF INFLUENCE

Somewhere along the way, the meaning of *influencer* got hijacked. What was once about impact has become about image. Influence was never supposed to be about selling detox tea or going viral for a trendy dance. It was meant to glorify God and guide people toward him.

So here's the reality check: We don't need more influencers chasing clout. We need more influencers chasing Christ.

It's time for us, sincere followers of Christ, to reclaim the true purpose of influence. Not for popularity, not for self-promotion, but for something far greater. And that starts with understanding what Christian influence is truly supposed to be.

1. Publicly share your belief in Jesus Christ. (No, not just in your Instagram bio—live it out loud.)
2. Live a life that exemplifies godly principles. (Your content should match your character.)
3. Never lose sight of the Great Commission. (Because Jesus didn't tell us to keep our faith to ourselves.)

Speaking of the Great Commission, let's look at what Jesus said. In Matthew 28:19-20 (ESV), he makes it crystal clear: "Go therefore and make disciples of all nations, baptizing them in the name of the Father and of the Son and of the Holy Spirit, teaching them to observe all that I have commanded you. And behold, I am with you always, to the end of the age."

Let's break this down:

- "Go therefore"—Don't sit still. Influence is active, not passive.
- "Make disciples"—Influence isn't about followers; it's about leading people to Christ.
- "Teach them to observe all that I have commanded you"—This isn't a "live your truth" situation. Jesus gave clear instructions, and part of influence is helping others live according to his Word.
- "I am with you always"—You're not doing this alone. Influence with faith, not fear.

The problem is, too many Christians have gotten comfortable staying silent. Maybe it's fear of criticism, fear of rejection, or fear of not being relatable. But Jesus never said, "Go and blend in with the crowd." He said, "Go and make disciples."

If we don't publicly share our faith, the world will publicly replace it with something else.

Publicly sharing our belief in Jesus is biblical but also practically endorses our faith in him. Studies show there has been a steady increase in the number of Americans who say they are atheists, agnostics, religiously unaffiliated, or believe "nothing in particular."[3] With every passing generation, more and more people are separating from Jesus. This is why it is even more

7

necessary that believers are vocal and visible with their faith. Some Christians might feel that sharing their beliefs publicly could negatively impact their careers. However, the Scriptures are clear on this: "If you are ashamed of me and of my teaching, then the Son of Man will be ashamed of you when he comes in his glory and in the glory of the Father and of the holy angels" (Luke 9:26 GNT). The consequences of not sharing our faith are far greater than those we might currently anticipate.

JOSEPH AND DAVID: TWO INFLUENCERS, TWO OUTCOMES

Joseph didn't ask to be an influencer. His circumstances positioned him for it. He was betrayed by his brothers, sold into slavery, and thrown into prison. By all accounts, he should have

been bitter, broken, or at the very least, silent. But instead, he let godly influence shape his story. His integrity and faith elevated him to a position where he could save an entire nation from famine (Genesis 41:39-41).

David, on the other hand, shows us that being an influencer doesn't require flawlessness. David made catastrophic mistakes, his sin with Bathsheba being one of the most infamous (2 Samuel 11). But his response to failure set him apart. Instead of deflecting blame, David repented wholeheartedly. His prayer in Psalm 51:10 is one of the most raw and sincere in the Bible: "Create in me a pure heart, O God, and renew a steadfast spirit within me."

David's humility and willingness to return to God remind us that true influence isn't about perfection. It's about authenticity and redemption.

WHAT'S NEXT?

If I'm going to encourage you to embrace vulnerability as an influencer, then it's only right that I lead by example. That's why, in the chapters that follow, I'll take you on my personal influencer journey: how I got here, what I had to sacrifice, and the unexpected lessons I learned along the way. Most people have seen my accomplishments and success, but very few know the real story behind them.

Next, we will dive into the secret ingredient that most people overlook when building an impactful social media platform. Spoiler alert: It has nothing to do with algorithms, aesthetics, or even viral content.

We'll also look at case studies of individuals who have successfully used their platforms to glorify God and make a lasting impact. You'll see firsthand what works, what doesn't, and what truly sets apart an effective Christian influencer.

Finally, we'll break down the four key components of influence and how you can use them to grow your platform, amplify your message, and walk boldly in your calling.

At the end of the day, influence is inevitable. The real question is, will your influence push people toward God or pull them away from him?

2

WHERE WE FIT IN

When I was a freshman in college, I created a profile on Facebook. At the time, social media was not yet widely adopted. Facebook was originally built for college students. You needed a college email address just to create a profile. Most users had no clue that this social networking system would become as impactful as it is today.

I remember creating my first profile on Facebook and thinking, *This is a lifesaver.* It was a great way to communicate with friends without wasting text messaging data. Back then, unlimited texting wasn't common. There also weren't very many opportunities for you to meet people outside of your campus community. The access that Facebook provided at the time allowed you to connect with other college students without ever leaving your dorm room. If you identified as an introvert, then you might have also found this opportunity to be a saving grace. Many introverts have very outgoing personalities but don't easily open up around people. As a freshman in college, I was nervous and reluctant to meet new people. Social media made it so much easier. For introverts like me it was a game changer. I figured out how to be social on social media while still maintaining my reserved nature in person.

In time, I gained a greater perspective of how people shape perceptions of the world. Unfortunately, this often leads individuals to lose their own identity and adopt personalities that aren't their own. Social media is a powerful tool that can be misused; we frequently see influencers presenting filtered lives far from reality. However, social media also offers the opportunity to observe individuals living authentically, providing inspiration and genuine influence.

I've had the pleasure of meeting influential people from all walks of life—political figures, actors, public speakers, theologians, and celebrities. Among them was my first millionaire mentor, Dr. Gicele Wray-Lindley, who became one of the most impactful figures in my life. She exemplified what is possible when you put God first and diligently pursue your craft.

MOST SUCCESSFUL PEOPLE DON'T START OFF TRYING TO BE THE BEST; THEY START BY DOING THEIR BEST.

Dr. Wray-Lindley was a distinguished pastor and entrepreneur in Chicago, a powerhouse who owned multiple businesses and still made time to pour into the lives of others. She was the kind of person who constantly seemed to be moving. She was always busy, yet she had a remarkable ability to pause and truly listen. Her support and knowledge were the foundation that helped me start my own business, something I might never have had the courage to do without her.

She was unapologetically blunt, and her honesty was a breath of fresh air. She kept it real, always telling you what you needed to hear rather than what you wanted to hear. But along with that straightforwardness came genuine care and a willingness to help. She didn't just give advice—she gave time, energy, and resources to support and uplift other entrepreneurs like myself.

Dr. Wray-Lindley's influence showed me what was possible when you merge faith, hard work, and an authentic commitment to helping others. When I personally struggled with believing I had what it took to be a person of influence, she was one of the people who pushed me to not limit myself. I was able to establish connections because I successfully utilized my platform to engage with the world.

Ironically, I became an influencer by accident. I didn't start by trying to reach the world. I was blessed with the opportunity to teach and work as an administrator at the same institution I once attended as an undergraduate student. Being connected in that way helped me to be intentional about giving back while I was on campus.

Working as a director of diversity at a Christian institution was one of the most challenging and rewarding experiences of my life. It also afforded me the opportunity to teach an entry-level course to college students. My initial goal for starting a social media page was to infiltrate the space where students spent most of their time and, hopefully, influence them to be more involved in the work that was important on campus. But I couldn't properly switch their attention until I first understood what they considered important. My goal quickly expanded once I realized the potential that social media really had. I never would have imagined that one day I would be speaking in rooms filled with thousands of individuals seeking to learn from me. I would love to take credit and say that my talent alone is what made it all possible. But I cannot. Anyone can duplicate the success I have acquired by unlocking the potential of social networking.

Social media is a window to the world. Not only can you use it to interact with your friends, but you can also use it to understand what's happening in the world. Oftentimes, my students would know about current events before I did. Rather than wait for the media to cover breaking news stories, you can see stories breaking as they are happening. When you look more closely at the value of social media, you see that its use is deeper and more far-reaching than you think. News outlets use social media to disseminate information because of social media's relevance and immediate impact on people. Outlets like *TMZ* and *The Shade Room* are known for their ability to share culturally relevant breaking news. So, understandably, more and more individuals are utilizing social media as their primary means of staying informed.

This realization led me to create a platform on which I branded myself as "Jackie the Educator." My platform talked about a wide range of subjects that kept my audience informed via social media. The topics were rarely, if ever, discussed elsewhere (or outside of social media platforms). I challenged my audience to think outside the box. I often talked about tough topics that were not allowed to be discussed on campus but were acceptable on a social platform. For example, among the controversial subjects we discussed were "Should Christians smoke weed?" and "understanding the LGBTQ community." One of the most iconic conversations on campus was during the Hillary Clinton versus Donald Trump presidential election. At the time, the campus was very divided. It was sometimes difficult to walk the line of being a college administrator and an influencer, but I managed to do both by presenting the facts that would allow individuals to come to their own conclusions. Doing so was often controversial for most faculty and staff on campus, but it deeply connected me to the students, many of whom became fans and avid supporters. Although I had successfully won the respect of the students on campus, I also sacrificed my reputation among many of the traditional faculty and staff. At the time, the utilization of social media for professionals was not widely accepted.

There has always been this unspoken rule that instructors and administrators must keep their personal lives private, never allowing students to know that they are humans who eat, sleep, poop, and make mistakes just like everyone else. As a young girl attending Burr Oak Middle School, I once saw one of my sixth-grade teachers at the grocery store checkout wearing a headscarf, holding a box of tampons, and sifting through the candy bars on display. For some reason that image changed how I interacted in her class. After seeing her in such a human light, I became less afraid to ask questions and even felt more comfortable sharing personal struggles.

Sometimes we become overly protective of our personal lives and deny people the ability to see how similar we actually are. Throughout my time in education, I would often hear about the potential risks of being too open on social media. These concerns were frequently voiced by individuals who grew up in a time when privacy was approached differently with a greater emphasis on safeguarding personal information. Many still prefer methods like paper bank statements because of concerns about information falling into the wrong hands. While their caution is understandable, it's worth considering that information has been falling into the wrong hands long before the advent of Facebook and Instagram.

Perhaps if we focused less on keeping certain parts of ourselves hidden and more on living authentically, we could foster greater consistency in our character. In my opinion, some people are hesitant to share the real version of themselves out of fear that others might misuse or misinterpret their openness. However, it is much harder to maintain a double life—constantly guarding or presenting only certain aspects of who you are—than it is to focus on being authentic in every room you step into.

My attempts to explain the relevance of social media to other faculty and staff were often met with judgmental criticism. In some of my colleagues' eyes, my effort to connect with students came across as attention seeking. To this day, it is still not uncommon for individuals to perceive social media platforms as unprofessional. Some industries strictly forbid employees to use social media in the workplace, while others are slowly coming around to the idea of it being a useful tool. Unfortunately, the appropriate utilization of social media will likely remain a debate for many years to come.

But here's what I've learned: Progress often comes from stepping outside of what's comfortable or widely accepted. Sometimes, challenging traditional narratives is the only way to create space for meaningful change. I encourage you to reflect on your own experiences, especially in professional settings, and consider how you can apply the lessons I've shared. What risks are you willing to take to connect with others in a way that feels authentic to you? What conversations can you initiate to bring fresh perspectives to the table? Don't be afraid to go against the grain, even if it means facing criticism. Change rarely happens by staying silent or conforming to outdated norms. Instead, let your willingness to challenge tradition inspire others to see things differently.

Thankfully, my journey did not end in an institutional setting. What I didn't know at the time was that my journey was just beginning. After establishing a base of supporters among students, my platform began to expand to all individuals seeking to think critically and expose themselves to different perspectives. Not long after my transition from higher education, I decided to start a YouTube show called *Higher Learning*. In my efforts to engage in thought-provoking dialogue, I invited guests who sometimes had controversial ideas. Again, as a believer, I realized that there were a lot of topics that some Christians deem inappropriate to discuss in a pulpit. So I decided to discuss them in a setting that had fewer restrictions or rules.

Although the idea of a show like this was interesting, I found myself actively thinking of ways to attract the right audience to these conversations. Most people struggle with finding the right audience for their content. I have seen countless people who have amazing ideas but struggle to reach their target market. This is what led me to create Black Christian Influencers (BCI). I distinctly remember sitting on a pew at my father's church and writing down my ideal target market. On that sheet of paper, I wrote down *millennials, educated, Christian, Black, leaders,* and *influencers.* After reviewing my list and thinking about the audience that I had already gathered through my social media platform, I landed on three words that stood out to me: *Black, Christian, influencers.* This was my target audience, and thus I created a community.

Black Christian Influencers started as a community of strangers who were brought together to facilitate conversations among Christians of like-mindedness. It slowly developed into a plethora of other ventures as I started to learn more about the members' individual needs. What started out as an effort to reach my target market developed into a larger concept that would allow others to reach *their* target audiences. Without much thought, I had created a community that was ful-

KEEPING YOUR PURPOSE IN MIND WILL HELP YOU TO STAY FOCUSED ON NOT JUST BEING MARKETABLE BUT BEING IMPACTFUL.

filling a need for so many others. I quickly understood the importance of establishing an impactful community. Many people become so consumed with their initial idea that they forget to remain open to a better one.

If we focus on the impact, we will always get results. Many people lose sight of that, which is why they end up too focused on the things that don't really matter. When I first started the community, I was scared because I lacked the experience that

I thought would be required to maintain an engaged network of people. It took me a while to figure out that I needed to be confident in my ability and not my experience. We will always have the opportunity to step out into the unknown. In those instances, it is important to allow ourselves to learn and grow from our own trial and error.

I am thankful for my season of developing my business because it gave me the experience that I desired. Learning these lessons required sacrifice. Whether you are pursuing a career, platform, or relationships, sacrifices will always be necessary. To reach my goal, I sacrificed my career as an educator. However, my career as an educator never really ended. I now get to educate people in a variety of ways. The sacrifice was worth the reward of seeing so many people impacted by the business—the community—I have built.

Developing your platform as an influencer opens the door to a plethora of other opportunities, whether it's public speaking, brand deals, or full-time ministry. Your time sacrificed to build a platform will be worth the investment. But to reach the reward, you must first get through the process of developing a social media platform. Thick skin is required. Social media is not exclusive to "good" people. You will likely encounter people who are disrespectful, lack integrity, and intentionally try to hinder your success.

When I first started my journey, I would get distracted by the opinions of individuals who I was not called to reach. Often, we are looking to please everyone when we should really only be focusing on our target audience. We have all seen or heard of instances when people who disagree on social media post hostile comments that hurt others. The unfortunate reality of social media is that even typed words have power. Even if you can't see the other person, the words they share are just as impactful. People have become comfortable with sharing thoughts that are intentionally harmful to others.

Building a platform isn't easy—it takes time, sacrifice, and the willingness to push through uncomfortable moments. There will be critics, distractions, and even moments when you question why you started. But those challenges aren't meant to stop you; they're meant to shape you.

At the end of the day, it's not about pleasing everyone or having the perfect platform. It's about staying true to your purpose and showing up for the people you are called to reach. Stay focused on the impact, trust the process, and don't let anything or anyone keep you from what you're meant to do.

3

MARKETING AND EXCELLENCE MATTER

L et's be real: Marketing is just a fancy word for getting people to care about what you're offering. It's about connecting the dots between what you have and what someone else needs. Whether it's selling a product, sharing a message, or spreading a mission, good marketing isn't about gimmicks—it's about making things click for the right audience at the right time.

When it comes to faith, marketing isn't just a strategy; it's part of the work. What's the gospel if not the ultimate message worth sharing? We've been doing it for centuries, whether we called it marketing or ministry. Jesus set the standard. His ability to reach people, connect deeply, and share transformative truths was nothing short of masterful. If we're going to talk about marketing done right, we've got to talk about Jesus.

JESUS THE MARKETER

Contrary to what some Christians might think, it is not a sin to market the gospel. Marketing has been part of Christianity since Jesus and his disciples walked the earth. Jesus was, without question, a brilliant communicator—and, if we're being honest, a marketing genius. He didn't call it marketing, of course, but he knew exactly how to connect with people and get his message across. Take his parables, for instance. They weren't just random stories; they were carefully crafted to package deep, spiritual truths into everyday scenarios that people could relate to. It was like he was saying, "Let me come to your level."

Jesus also had a knack for knowing his audience. Whether he was talking to fishermen, tax collectors, or religious leaders, he adapted his examples to fit their lives. To fishermen, he spoke about casting nets and catching fish; to farmers, he talked about sowing seeds. He had a personalized approach for every crowd he faced, making his message hit home. And don't forget his personal brand. His authenticity and compassion were undeniable. Everywhere he went, people could feel that he genuinely cared, which is why his message stuck.

Then there was his team strategy. Jesus didn't just build a following; he built a movement by empowering his disciples to share the message with him. They were like the first brand ambassadors, spreading what he taught them to the people in their circles. From his miracles to his one-on-one conversations, Jesus gave them more than enough material to share. His value proposition was clear: freedom, healing, and salvation.

THE ART OF MODERN-DAY EVANGELISM

Marketing and ministry have always been connected. In today's digital world, sharing faith-driven content is like modern-day evangelism. Whether through storytelling, social media, or public speaking, the goal is the same: meeting people where they are and making the message clear, relevant, and impactful.

WHAT'S YOUR MINISTRY MESSAGE?

Every influencer, entrepreneur, or thought leader has a "gospel" they share—their core message. Jesus understood that clarity, connection, and consistency move people to action. As you build your platform, consider:

- Who is your audience, and how do they best receive information?
- How can you present your message in a way that resonates deeply?
- Are you making it easy for people to connect and engage with your mission?

From the hillside to the timeline, engagement is key. Jesus mastered connection long before algorithms appeared. How can you follow his lead?

Even Jesus' choice of venues was strategic. He didn't stay tucked away in private corners—he went where the people were. Mountainsides, marketplaces, and even fishing boats became his stage. His actions and teachings were so memorable that people couldn't help but talk about them. You might say he was the master of word-of-mouth marketing before it was even a thing.

What set Jesus apart, though, was his ability to connect emotionally. He didn't just tell people what they needed to hear—he made them feel it. He saw people for who they truly were, met them in their struggles, and gave them hope. His message transformed lives. More than a teacher or a healer, he was a revolutionary marketer who showed us that connection, authenticity, and a little bit of strategy can change the world.

Marketing is bigger than TV ads and profit-generating campaigns. Marketing is the driving force behind how most people make decisions. Every day we make decisions influenced by things we have heard or seen. From the toothpaste we use to the hairstyles we wear, we have been marketed to and influenced by things outside of ourselves. Jesus used marketing to save the world. He not only marketed the gospel during his earthly ministry, but he also uses the written word to spread the hope of salvation to every man and woman who has an ear to hear. Purpose motivated Jesus to stay focused on his message.

We need purpose in order to not lose sight of what we are called to do. It is not uncommon for individuals to struggle with finding purpose on social media. Our exposure to so much thoughtless content has hurt our ability to create and recognize meaningful content. To create purposeful content, we must first explore our passions and find the real message that we are called to share. This message can evolve and grow just as we do. Exploring our passions requires time alone to reflect on what makes us special. The daily distractions of life and constant consumption of others' opinions and perspectives can make it difficult to decipher between our own thoughts and those of others. This is why taking time to think and pray alone is imperative. When Jesus was fulfilling his purpose, he often took time away from his disciples and followers to be alone (see Mark 1:35 and Luke 5:16). His time alone kept him focused on the assignment.

PURPOSE COMES WITH PAIN

As much as I would like to assure you that this journey of self-discovery will be exhilarating and joyful, it might lead you through some painful moments. Oftentimes, our greatest purpose is connected to our greatest pain—the place where we have our highest level of expertise. Our experience gives us a unique viewpoint of specific scenarios. We can speak more passionately about subjects we've lived through than those we haven't. For example, breast cancer survivors can speak to a newly diagnosed patient about the struggles of recovery and treatment far better than someone who has never experienced them.

Before I started my influencer organization, I was close with someone who was influential. He was an artist whose reach and audience were growing rapidly. We had so much in common that he felt like my best friend at one point. However, his growing influence introduced challenges and dynamics I didn't fully understand.

During one difficult conversation, he shared that his life was beginning to change in ways that made it hard for us to stay on the same page. He was dealing with complexities I couldn't yet comprehend. His expanding platform brought not only success but also a set of pressures that were unfamiliar to me at the time. When our relationship ended, I was devastated. I didn't understand why we couldn't continue to support each other through this new season of his life.

That loss, though painful, became a pivotal moment for me. It felt like my world had shifted, but over time, I began to see how it prepared me for my own journey. Without that pain, I might not have fully embraced my calling to help influencers and build an organization that supports people much like the friend I once had. That experience gave me a deeper understanding of the challenges that come with influence and equipped me to serve others who are walking similar paths. What felt like rejection at the time ultimately positioned me for the work I do now.

Having now experienced my own level of exponential growth, I recognize just how much one's life changes when one steps into the public eye. As an introvert and recovering overthinker, I've learned how challenging it can be to navigate relationships when you start questioning the motives of those around you. It becomes harder to trust, and you realize you can no longer speak or act as freely as you once did. Your words and actions are always being observed and are often misinterpreted.

Through that experience, I came to understand the weight my friend was carrying. The constant judgment, the pressure to perform, and the isolation that come with influence can be overwhelming. At the time, I didn't grasp the emotional toll of living under that kind of scrutiny—how private pain becomes public commentary and how exhausting it can be to relive your struggles through the lens of strangers' opinions.

The lessons I've gained from that season weren't easy, but they've given me a new perspective and a deeper empathy for others navigating similar journeys. I've also learned the importance of staying grounded in my purpose. Influence can be draining, but when you remain focused on the "why" behind your calling, it becomes easier to persevere.

Finding ways to stay focused on your assignment is even more important. We are called to do great things, but sometimes that calling comes at a cost. Nevertheless, we cannot be afraid to harness our pain and use it for the glory of God. One thing I've learned through this journey is that pain is never wasted. It can shape us, strengthen us, and prepare us to help others walking similar paths. Losing that friendship was hard, but it gave me the perspective and drive I needed to step into my calling. What once felt like an ending became the foundation for the work I do and the purpose I now embrace.

Even though the process might feel overwhelming at times, there's nothing more fulfilling than seeing the fruits of your labor. God has a way of taking every mistake, every heartbreak, and every struggle and using it for good. Some of the most inspirational people we see online today didn't get to where they are without going through some serious challenges.

Take Tabitha Brown, for example. She spent over twenty years chasing her dreams in Hollywood, but nothing seemed to work out the way she had hoped. She experienced countless setbacks, struggles, and moments when she could've given up. But instead, she leaned into her faith and kept going. It wasn't until she started sharing her authentic self—her faith, her journey, and her love for vegan food—that everything began to fall into place. Now, she's a household name, inspiring millions with her story of perseverance and grace.

Or think about Kevin Fredericks, better known as KevOnStage. He started out performing comedy at church talent nights and slowly grew his audience online. He wasn't some overnight success story—he put in years of work, faced rejection, and wrestled with self-doubt along the way. But his authenticity and ability to connect with people have made him one of the most relatable and loved comedians today. Both

Tabitha and Kevin are reminders that the struggles we face can become the very things that fuel our purpose.

Looking at my own journey, I see the same pattern. When I first started my business, I doubted if I had what it took to bring the vision God gave me to life. Even now, there are moments when self-doubt creeps in. But I've realized that sharing my struggles as an entrepreneur—my fears, my insecurities, and even my failures—has been one of the most impactful things I've done. At first, I thought being vulnerable made me look weak, but I've learned it's a strength. The very things I used to hide are the things that resonate with people the most.

That said, I've also had to learn the importance of discernment. A friend once explained the difference between being transparent and being opaque. Transparency is about sharing vulnerably, while being opaque means sharing with wisdom—being intentional about how much and what you reveal. Not everyone needs to know every detail of your journey, and that's okay. People can still see your heart and feel your authenticity without you overexposing yourself.

Looking back, I can see how God has used every insecurity, mistake, and moment of self-doubt to inspire others. That's why I believe no part of your journey should go to waste. The things you've been through, even the hardest parts, can bring a deeper connection and understanding to those you're called to reach. You don't have to have it all together, just a willingness to share what God has done and is still doing in your life. That's what makes the journey worth it.

PINPOINT YOUR PURPOSE

Discovering your purpose isn't just about knowing what you're good at—it's about committing to growth. A growth mindset means understanding that your skills, talents, and potential aren't set in stone; they expand with effort and experience. Some people juggle multiple gifts

> FEAR BURIES POTENTIAL. WHETHER IT'S IN THE GROUND OR IN YOUR DRAFTS FOLDER, WASTED TALENT HELPS NO ONE.

like a pro, while others are laser-focused on one calling. Either way, the assignment remains the same: Maximize what God has given you and use it well.

Let's clear up a common misconception. When Jesus told the parable of the talents (Matthew 25:14-30), he wasn't talking about skills like singing, speaking, or leading. He was talking about *money*. The Greek word *talanton* (τάλαντον) refers to a large sum of currency. But here's where it gets interesting: While the parable is literally about financial investment, the lesson runs deeper. It's about what we do with *any* resource God entrusts to us, whether that's money, skills, influence, or opportunities.

In the story, a wealthy man hands his three servants different amounts of money. One gets five talents, another gets two, and the last guy gets just one. The first two go all in, invest wisely, and double their money. But the third panics, digs a hole, and buries his talent in the ground like a squirrel hiding nuts for winter. Spoiler alert: The boss is *not* impressed.

The moral? Although it is tempting to hide our value out of fear of rejection, we must remember that hidden talents serve no purpose. Whether you have five gifts or just one, don't let fear keep you from using them.

THE STAGES OF EXCELLENCE

Growth is imperative to our success. We must constantly adapt to the changing world around us, especially when it comes to digital technology. What was effective marketing ten years ago is now obsolete. We have to continually educate ourselves and evolve with the times. This consistent pursuit of growth is known as excellence. We should all strive to deliver the best versions of ourselves that we possibly can, as this will enable us to reach the people we are assigned to reach. The pursuit of excellence involves at least four stages centered around the following areas: target audience, expertise, strategy, and content.

STAGE ONE—FIND A TARGET AUDIENCE. Reaching our target market requires focus, strategy, and intentionality. One thing many people struggle with on their social media journey is finding their target audience. The problem is that most people haven't even identified who their target audience is. To successfully find the people you are assigned to, you must start by taking an assessment of the types of people who are drawn to you. I believe that we are all called to reach specific people. Oftentimes we want to choose our audience, but the reality is that our audience chooses us. Start by asking questions to the individuals who find your platform valuable. If you have not yet started a platform, ask the people you encounter regularly. Here are some questions you should ask:

1. Can you share a time that I helped you with a problem?
2. What are some things you think I am good at?
3. What are three words you would use to describe me?
4. If I started a business, what do you think it would be?
5. What value have I added to your life?

These questions are meant to draw out what people perceive as your value. Learning what others find valuable about you will help you to understand your target market better. It might also reveal that those people who you thought were your target audience are more your support system rather than your consumers.

You will likely find that there is a specific type of person who is drawn to what you do. For example, I have often been told that I explain difficult subjects in a simple manner. Thus, individuals who are eager to learn are naturally drawn to me. Your target audience isn't based solely on typical demographic descriptions of age, race, and gender. Target audiences can be based on occupations, religion, educational background, hobbies, learning styles, and so much more.

Be cautious about assuming that your target audience consists of people who are just like you. I see so many people make the mistake of trying to target individuals who only have the same interests as them. For instance, a musician could easily assume that the people who will buy their album are limited to music lovers like themselves. However, musicians who become successful have found a way to connect with individuals they might never have suspected to be interested.

Some target audiences are solely connected based on style, experience, and point of view. You must have a strategy in place to find these individuals. Before social media, it was a lot harder for people to reach new audiences due to the control of gate-keepers who held access to large stages. If you didn't have the right connections, you were not granted access. Now, because of social media, we can bypass those gatekeepers and find our own audiences to connect with.

STAGE TWO—FOCUS ON EXPERTISE. To establish yourself as a go-to person in your field, you need to focus on a specific area of expertise. Doing so can be challenging for those who are multi-talented and have various aspects of their story that others find inspiring. For example, I am a mother, an entrepreneur, a teacher, and—depending on the time of year—a health enthusiast. However, at times, I might focus solely on my entrepreneurial endeavors so that my audience clearly sees me as an expert in that space.

The goal of focusing isn't to limit your abilities but to channel them in a way that makes them more digestible for your au-dience. Think of a funnel: It starts wide at the top and narrows at the end. Now, picture your audience as a bottle with a small opening. If you try to pour everything in at once without a funnel, much of what you share won't make it in. But when you use a funnel to focus your content, you ensure that your message reaches your audience without overwhelming them.

Focusing also helps you to pace yourself. Timing is just as important as the messages you share. Many people start strong with their marketing efforts but burn out quickly. The key isn't to produce massive amounts of content but to maintain con-sistency over time.

STAGE THREE—STRATEGIZE FOR RESULTS. Focus is great, but without a strategy, you're just throwing spaghetti at the wall and hoping something sticks. Whether you're a preacher, entrepreneur, or fashion influencer, you need a game plan to make an impact.

Most people assume the goal of social media is to rack up likes and follows like it's a competition. But the goal is to build real connections, ones that extend beyond the algorithm-controlled walls of social media. As powerful as social platforms are, they can be unpredictable. One day your post is blowing up, the next day it's crickets. Why? The ever-changing social media algorithm.

Think of the algorithm as a finicky restaurant critic deciding which dishes (a.k.a. content) make it to the top of the menu. It's a complex system that ranks, filters, and selects what people see. Since these rules are always shifting, you can't rely solely on social media to reach your people. That's why you need to be strategic about building a community outside of social media.

Create spaces you can control. If you want to stay connected to your audience without an algorithm playing middleman, you need spaces that you own. Here are some foolproof ways to do just that:

- Email lists—Yep, email is still king. If Instagram disappeared tomorrow, you'd still have direct access to your audience. Services like Mailchimp or ConvertKit make it easy.
- Text message communities—Platforms like Community, SimpleTexting, or WhatsApp let you text updates, send

reminders, or even deliver exclusive content straight to people's phones.

- Your own website or blog—Think of this as your digital headquarters. If someone googles you, this is where they should land.
- Membership platforms—Want to offer premium content? Services like Patreon, Substack, or even a private Facebook group create exclusive spaces where your biggest supporters can engage with you.
- Podcasting—If you've got something to say, start a podcast. No algorithm will bury your message, and you can build a loyal audience over time.

Create a funneling system. You need a smooth way to guide people from your social media to your owned spaces. This is called a funnel. One of the easiest ways is through your link in bio. Your bio should have a clear, easy-to-navigate link that takes people where you want them to go, whether it's your email list, a landing page, or a shop. Tools like Linktree, Beacons, or a direct website link help organize multiple destinations in one spot. Don't make people hunt for ways to connect with you— make it easy!

Set SMART goals.

- Winging it is not a strategy. You need goals that mean something. Enter SMART goals: specific, measurable, attainable, relevant, and time-bound.
- An example SMART goal for an influencer is, "Increase my Instagram engagement rate from 2 percent to 4 percent in the next three months by posting five high-quality reels

per week and responding to 90 percent of comments within twenty-four hours." This goal keeps your growth intentional instead of just posting and praying.[1]

Review your social media metrics. Your analytics are like report cards for your content by telling you what's working and what's flopping. Data on engagement rate, reach, and impressions help you work smarter, not harder.

Pick the right social media platform. You don't need to be everywhere—you just need to be where your audience is. Here's a cheat sheet:

- Instagram and TikTok—great for visual content and younger audiences
- LinkedIn—your playground if you're a thought leader or business pro
- Facebook groups—perfect for community-driven engagement
- YouTube and podcasts—ideal for long-form content and deep dives

The bottom line: Go where your people already are and master that platform.

Research other influencers in your niche. Success leaves clues. If you want to know what works, study influencers with similar audiences. What are they doing well? Where are they getting engagement? How are they interacting with their followers?

This doesn't mean copying—it means learning and adapting strategies that fit your unique brand.

The key to winning on social media? Be intentional. There's no one-size-fits-all approach to social media success. What works for someone else might not work for you, and that's okay.

But one thing is universal: Posting without a plan is a waste of time. Your audience needs value, consistency, and connection. While it's totally fine to post a funny meme, a random thought, or a behind-the-scenes moment, don't lose sight of your purpose.

At the end of the day, purpose keeps you going when the likes slow down, the algorithm shifts, and comparison creeps in. Stay strategic and consistent and watch your influence grow.

STAGE FOUR—CREATE CONTENT THAT CONNECTS. Most of us struggle with content. Think of your content as the way your audience will decide if they want to enter a committed relationship with you (as in follow your page). Before I tell you what meaningful content is, I will tell you what it is *not*. Advertising with a flyer on your page for your upcoming event is *not* meaningful content. Posting a picture with the cover of your new book is *not* meaningful content. These types of content are meant to promote something that has already been proven valuable. Before you can promote something, you must first show the consistent value of your work.

When you are creating content, you need to first brainstorm all the ways you can add value to your audience. Don't limit yourself to tips and strategies; think of ways you can share your testimony, successes, and progression of platform expansion. When people look for new influencers to follow and support, they want to be a part of your journey, not just your arrival. Be intentional with sharing not only the positive sides of what you deal with but also the bumpy roads and hidden complications.

One of the best ways to connect with your audience is to include them in the process. When I first became an influencer, I often shared aspects of my life that were still developing. I had recently started a business and didn't have all the answers. I didn't know how to write a business plan or market an event, or even how to monetize. However, I was very intentional in sharing my journey with my audience.

As you continue to share your journey, consider incorporating interactive elements into your content such as these:

- Conduct live Q&A sessions in which your audience can directly engage with you by asking questions about your experiences and seeking advice. Doing so not only builds a sense of community but also allows your followers to feel more connected to your journey.

- Share personal stories related to your endeavors, struggles, and triumphs. Craft narratives that resonate emotionally with your audience, making your content not just informative but deeply relatable. This emotional connection can be a driving force in building a loyal and engaged following.

- Explore different content formats to keep your platform interesting. Incorporate short video clips and even guest features to diversify your content offerings. Doing so not only caters to various preferences but also showcases your adaptability in the digital landscape.

- As you dive into these strategies, remember the essence of excellence. Consistently refine your content, keeping it aligned with your purpose and goals. By adhering to these principles, you will not only enrich your audience's experience but also establish a lasting impact in the ever-evolving world of social media marketing.

- Share behind-the-scenes glimpses of your daily life and work routine to humanize your online presence. This transparency allows your audience to see the person behind the brand, making your content more relatable. Whether it's a snapshot of your workspace, your daily rituals, or snippets of your creative process, these insights create a sense of connection that goes beyond the digital interface.

- As you progress, explore multimedia content such as podcasts or webinars. These formats provide an opportunity for in-depth discussions, allowing you to share valuable insights, interview industry experts, and connect with your audience on a more personal level. The versatility of multimedia content caters to diverse learning preferences, accommodating a broader audience.

- Think of hashtags as digital breadcrumbs leading new audiences straight to your content. To get the best results, mix popular hashtags (such as #Motivation) with niche-specific ones (such as #FaithDrivenBusiness) to attract the right crowd. Keep it clean; five to ten well-chosen hashtags work better than a chaotic hashtag dump. Create a branded hashtag to build community and make it easy for followers to engage with your content. Stay ahead of the game by tracking trending hashtags with tools like Hashtagify or RiteTag. And don't just slap hashtags anywhere—test whether they perform better in captions or comments to maximize engagement.

Social media moves quickly. Blink, and the algorithm has changed again. To stay ahead, you need to keep your finger on the pulse of platform updates, trends, and new features. Follow industry blogs like Social Media Examiner and HubSpot, tune into webinars from Meta Blueprint or LinkedIn Learning, and track engagement shifts with tools like Sprout Social and BuzzSumo. The more you learn, the more quickly you can adapt, pivot, and thrive. In a digital world where trends fade as quickly as they appear, the real influencers aren't just reacting—they're staying two steps ahead.

As your audience grows, nurture the relationships you have built. Engage in conversations by responding to comments and direct messages. Foster a sense of community by acknowledging your followers and celebrating their milestones. This interactive approach not only strengthens your connection with existing followers but also attracts new ones drawn to the positive atmosphere surrounding your platform. Consider incorporating user-generated content into your strategy. Encourage your followers to share their experiences with your products or insights inspired by your content. Doing so diversifies your content and fosters a collaborative community where everyone feels valued and heard.

As mentioned earlier, meaningful content goes beyond surface-level promotion. Flyers and event promotion are considered surface-level content. Strive for a balance between content that is educational, inspirational, and entertaining. Your platform should be a blend of valuable insights, motivational stories, and moments of lightheartedness. This variety caters to different audience needs, ensuring your content remains engaging and diverse.

Don't be afraid to integrate your faith journey into your content. Share how your beliefs and values influence your entrepreneurial endeavors. Whether it's through quotes, reflections, or personal stories, weaving spirituality into your narrative adds depth and authenticity. This transparency allows your audience to connect with both your professional and spiritual journeys.

As you continue to refine your approach, stay true to your purpose, engage with your community, and embrace the ever-evolving nature of the digital landscape. Your commitment to excellence and meaningful content will not only cultivate a loyal following but also leave a lasting impact in the realm of social media marketing—and in the lives of those you share the gospel message with.

4

INNOVATION REQUIRED

There is a process to excellence. If everyone could just wake up and be the best version of themselves, the world would not be half as interesting and enjoyable. The process it takes to get to excellence is the journey of life. From the moment we are born until the day we die, we should be on a path of continual improvement and growth.

Some of us reach our peak early, while others push past plateaus and excel to new heights. As a youth I competed in speech competitions. When I started, I was extremely shy and often allowed my fear to overtake me. One time I was so overcome with fear that I began to cry while delivering a speech in front of a room full of people and judges. But as much as I wanted to run out of the room and hide, I pushed through my tears and delivered the speech. It was definitely not my best and was probably impossible to understand. Nevertheless, the success in that moment was not my delivery but my persistence to continue after failure.

Many of us struggle with persistence, especially when we attempt to do things that are not easy for us. Our instinct of preservation sometimes prevents us from exposing ourselves to uncomfortable situations. However, without that moment of failure I experienced, I would never have evolved into a speaker who went on to win regional- and state-level speech competitions. Pushing past fear is the main component in the evolution of excellence.

However, pushing past fear sounds a bit like a cliché and may even seem easy to those who don't understand how complex fear can be. Many people think fear is big and scary, but sometimes fear is the unknown. Think about it: Fear is often made known when a person experiences something for the first time. While first-time experiences that are good often become memories we try to mimic throughout our life, first-time experiences that are bad can easily become traumatic events and lifelong fears. Having experienced many traumatic events, I am well aware that fear can become incapacitating if you allow it to grow and never attempt to overcome it.

FEAR IS THE ENEMY OF INNOVATION. OUR FEARS HOLD US BACK FROM CREATING AND EXPERIENCING NEW IDEAS AND INSIGHTS.

Yet on the other side of fear is a world of innovation and opportunity.

In the world of influencers, fear often looks like holding ourselves back by duplicating what we see others do instead of creating our own way. It's easier to redo something you already know has been accepted rather than create something that doesn't already have a blueprint.

As the CEO of an organization that focuses on developing influencers and people who desire to grow their influence, I have always enjoyed watching people grow as they learn new things. It's one of the reasons why I have always been drawn to education. I've had the pleasure of coaching and teaching thousands of individuals from around the world and sharing my knowledge about influencers with them. As much as I love teaching large groups, I especially enjoy connecting with and coaching individuals. Some of the people I coached have gone on to become influencers with a reach of more than one million followers. They didn't start off that way, though. Most began with a platform that was budding with potential but hadn't yet found its unique voice.

One young woman I worked with named Danielle was a pastor full of energy with big ideas and a bold approach to discussing topics that many people shy away from. When we first met, her platform had fewer than five thousand followers, but I was immediately drawn to her ability to connect with her audience on a deeper level. She was already on the path to becoming a unique innovator—her strong biblical knowledge was paired with a natural comedic flair that made her stand out. However, despite her potential, she struggled to find her voice on social media.

Danielle was known as a traditional pastor outside of social media, but I could see that she had so much untapped creativity waiting to be fully expressed. Being in this position is a common struggle for many creatives. We often feel confined by the personas we've established in our communities, fearing that any deviation from what people expect will lead to rejection.

About 90 percent of the influencers I've worked with have told me they possess multiple skills and passions but struggle to decide how to showcase them. This is especially true for those in leadership, whether in corporate settings, personal brands, or ministry-related work. The expectations placed on leaders can make them feel boxed in and hesitant to break out. Danielle was no different.

During one of our conversations, I asked her why she wasn't showcasing more of her comedic voice on social media. In person, she was naturally witty and quick on her feet, and she had a way of making people laugh while simultaneously making them think. But on her social media platform, that aspect of her personality was almost nonexistent. Her content leaned heavily into theological discourse—valuable, but not fully reflective of who she was. She admitted that she worried about how people would perceive her if she blended humor with ministry.

After some coaching, we discovered that she didn't need to abandon her theological depth to embrace her humor; she needed to combine them. That's when she started experimenting with a character that would change everything: a humorous yet insightful depiction of God.

Danielle put on a pair of glasses, looked straight into the camera, and, with a mix of sarcasm and wisdom, responded to people's everyday struggles as if she were God himself. In one of her first viral videos, she reenacted a modern-day conversation between God and a believer who kept asking for a "sign," even though God had already given that person multiple signs.

"God, if this is really what you want me to do, just send me a clear sign!"

Cue Danielle, now in character, adjusting her glasses and responding with a deadpan expression: "I literally sent you three signs. The sermon, the text from your friend, and that random stranger who told you exactly what you needed to hear. What else do you want? A billboard?"

The video blew up. People flooded the comments.

"This is literally me—God is probably so tired of me asking for signs!"

"Why do I feel so convicted and entertained at the same time?"

"I never thought about it this way, but this really makes me see how often I ignore what God is trying to tell me."

This shift in her content required her to tune out those who disagreed with her approach and focus on the people who were truly being blessed by her message. It wasn't easy. Making a shift like this sometimes means losing the core audience you've grown accustomed to. But you need to ask yourself: Is the risk of changing worth the reward of connecting with the people who truly need my voice?

Change can be scary, but it's also necessary. As Christians, we must constantly remind ourselves of who we are called to serve. If reaching people requires us to explore new methods, we need to be open to them. It's easy to stay in our comfort zones, encouraging the same audience with familiar content—but if that content isn't bearing fruit, we need to reassess our focus.

The reality is that many people spend more time scrolling on social media than they do sitting in church. That's why Danielle's shift in strategy made her even more effective. The pulpit is powerful, but social media allows for a different kind of reach—one that meets people where they already are. While sermons require an audience's dedicated time and attention, social media demands content that is engaging, relatable, and entertaining.

Many assume that influencers are shallow or superficial, but influencing is often harder than teaching. While teaching is a structured process where knowledge is willfully received, influence requires people to be unknowingly persuaded, or drawn in by content that resonates with them before they even realize they're learning something. As a former educator, I noticed early on that influencing and teaching have similar dynamics. Teaching happens in a controlled environment, while influence happens organically in moments when people least expect to be impacted.

Danielle eventually found her rhythm, stepping outside of her comfort zone and embracing a content style that was both thought provoking and humorous. Her audience responded in ways she never imagined. People began asking deeper questions about Scripture, engaging in meaningful discussions, and even sharing her videos to introduce biblical truths to their friends.

Of course, not everyone embraced her shift. Some felt her approach was too unconventional. But what mattered most was that she opened the door for a new wave of Christian content creators who desired to reach audiences in innovative ways. Two years later, Danielle—once an unsure pastor with a small following—now has more than a million followers and continues to blaze a trail for other faith-based influencers.

Her journey illustrates the transformative power of thinking outside the box and embracing innovation. If you want to elevate your influence, you have to be willing to do the same. Innovation means challenging conventional norms and finding new ways to present your message. It requires recognizing your strengths and learning how to blend them in a way that resonates with both you and your audience.

The remainder of this chapter will explore two more case studies and dive deeper into key principles that every aspiring influencer should embrace: vulnerability, digital adaptability, strategic storytelling, and understanding the true metrics of success.

THE POWER OF VULNERABILITY

Innovation is not limited to traditional ministry; it extends into every aspect of life. While overseeing an organization with thousands of influencers, I've had the privilege of witnessing some truly remarkable success stories. One that stood out was a mother—let's call her Rebecca—who was raising a son with a developmental disability and had a deep desire to build a community for parents like her. Rebecca's journey is a powerful example of how embracing innovation, particularly through vulnerability, can transform not only an individual's platform but also the lives of those they serve.

For a long time, I watched Rebecca create content that was both empowering and inspirational. However, despite the value she was providing, her content often struggled to gain traction. Why? People didn't know who she was or why they should listen to her. This is a common issue for many content creators. They assume that sharing valuable messages alone is enough to draw an audience. Yet it takes more than just offering value. It requires engaging, connecting, and even entertaining before people are willing to receive what you have to say.

When I talk about engagement, I don't just mean responding to comments or interacting with followers. I'm also talking about how you put yourself out there. Too often, content creators sit and wait for an audience to come to them when they should be actively going to their audience, meeting them where they already are. Rebecca was making the mistake of producing more and more content without truly engaging with the world around her. She poured so much effort into her posts only to see them fall flat.

Eventually, frustration set in. She had reached a crossroads: either keep doing the same thing and expect different results, or step out of her comfort zone and try something new. This time, she chose the latter. One day, she picked up her camera and, instead of crafting another perfectly polished post, she spoke from the heart. She openly shared the struggles of being a stay-at-home mom to a child with a disability—the feelings of isolation, the self-doubt, the moments when she questioned her worth. Midway through, she broke down in tears. It wasn't scripted. It wasn't planned. It was real. And that moment of raw vulnerability changed everything.

That video went viral.

People resonated with her honesty in a way that her previous content never achieved. Suddenly, the same audience she had struggled to reach was not only listening but also relating to her. Parents who felt the same struggles flooded her comments, thanking her for saying what they had been afraid to express.

By sharing her truth, Rebecca didn't just gain followers—she built a community.

Today, the very people she once struggled to reach are attending her conferences, reading her books, and investing in the resources she provides. By stepping outside of her box and embracing her personal story, she turned what once felt like a weakness into her greatest strength. She showed that true influence isn't about being perfect but about being real.

Rebecca's journey serves as a reminder that sometimes, the key to unlocking your audience isn't in doing more—it's in being more yourself. Authenticity is the bridge that connects you to the people who need your message the most. The moment you embrace that, your influence will naturally expand.

It's essential to reemphasize that the goal of innovation is not necessarily fame but rather mastery of your craft. It's about being exceptionally good at what you do, whether it's ministry, content creation, or any other endeavor. By focusing on excellence and embracing innovation, you can create a lasting impact and foster genuine connections with your audience. Innovation in Christian influence requires a departure from conventional norms, a willingness to embrace vulnerability, and a commitment to excellence.

Danielle's journey exemplifies the transformative power of breaking away from traditional ministry structures. By stepping beyond the pulpit and into a creative approach that blended theology with humor, she reached an entirely new audience that may have otherwise tuned her out. Her willingness to embrace a fresh, unconventional method—portraying God in a relatable and engaging way—allowed her to make biblical truth more accessible and impactful.

Similarly, Rebecca's story demonstrates how vulnerability can be a powerful tool for connection. As a mother navigating the challenges of raising a child with a disability, she initially struggled to gain traction with her content. But when she let go of polished perfection and shared her raw, unfiltered experiences, everything changed. Her openness resonated deeply with others facing similar struggles, allowing her to build a thriving, supportive community.

Both of these examples illustrate that true innovation isn't just about creativity—it's about authenticity. Whether it's reimagining how the gospel is shared or creating a space for people to feel seen and understood, innovation thrives when we embrace who we are and lean into what makes us unique. When we prioritize connection over convention, we not only expand our influence but also ensure that our impact is both meaningful and lasting.

As you navigate your own path of innovation, I encourage you to step outside the box, recognize your strengths, and find a successful mixture of perceived and observed strengths. Testing new approaches and staying attuned to audience feedback are integral components of the innovation process.

Innovation often emerges from the crucible of challenges. It is during moments of adversity that individuals are forced to think beyond their comfort zones, leading to creative solutions that can redefine their influence. Many content creators struggle with balancing personal hardships while maintaining an engaging and impactful presence. Whether it's navigating shifting audience expectations, overcoming self-doubt, or managing external pressures, these challenges often serve as the catalyst for transformation.

A common misconception is that success comes from a perfectly curated, uninterrupted journey. In reality, some of the most effective influencers allow their struggles to shape their message rather than silence it. When creators embrace transparency and vulnerability, their content often resonates on a deeper level, fostering a sense of connection that cannot be manufactured. Audiences are drawn not just to expertise but to relatability. Seeing someone wrestle with real issues and emerge stronger makes the message more compelling.

Difficulties, rather than being mere roadblocks, can spark creativity and resilience. Many influencers find that their most significant breakthroughs came not from carefully planned strategies but from the moments when they chose to share an unfiltered, authentic experience. Instead of viewing adversity as a hindrance, those who embrace it as part of their story often unlock new levels of impact, proving that innovation is not just about having fresh ideas but also about having the courage to grow through challenges.

ADAPTABILITY IN THE DIGITAL LANDSCAPE

We all need to be willing to adapt. The digital landscape is an ever-evolving arena, continuously presenting influencers with new challenges. Those seeking to remain relevant must adapt swiftly to changes, be they shifts in social media algorithms or emerging trends. The ability to innovate in response to these dynamics is essential for sustained success. For instance, one influencer, faced with drastic changes in social media algorithms, reimagined their content strategy. By staying informed and agile, they not only retained their audience but also attracted new followers. This adaptability underscores the importance of innovation as a fundamental component in navigating the digital age.

Innovation is rarely a solitary endeavor. Influencers often draw inspiration from diverse sources, making collaboration a vital aspect of their creative process. Exploring the dynamics of collaborative spaces reveals how influencers can leverage collective creativity to foster innovation. In today's interconnected digital world, collaborative platforms allow influencers to engage with like-minded individuals, creating communities centered around shared values and goals. These spaces serve as incubators for innovative ideas, enabling influencers to exchange insights and perspectives.[1]

STRATEGIC STORYTELLING: THE ART OF IMPACTFUL COMMUNICATION

At the heart of innovation lies the art of storytelling. The way influencers craft and communicate their narratives is pivotal in capturing their audience's attention and fostering connection. Delving into the elements of strategic storytelling adds another layer to our exploration of innovation. Influencers who excel in this realm understand the importance of weaving personal experiences, relatable anecdotes, and powerful visuals into their narratives. By creating a compelling tapestry, they captivate and inspire their audience.

An analysis of a renowned influencer known for impactful storytelling reveals the intentional choices made in their narrative construction. Their storytelling transcends mere messaging; it creates shared experiences that engage their audience on a deeper level, emphasizing the influential role of storytelling in the innovation process.[2]

INNOVATION METRICS: NAVIGATING SUCCESS IN THE DIGITAL REALM

As I discussed in chapter three, understanding the metrics of success in the digital realm is essential for sustaining innovation. By examining how influencers measure their impact, we gain insights into the tangible outcomes of their innovative strategies. While likes and follows are often seen as traditional markers of success, forward-thinking influencers recognize the need for a more nuanced approach. Engaging with metrics that reflect audience interaction, conversion rates, and the longevity of impact provides a comprehensive understanding of success.

Innovation within the realm of Christian influence is a multifaceted journey, encompassing passion, purpose, resilience, collaboration, strategic storytelling, and navigating digital metrics. By embracing these elements, influencers can cultivate a culture of continuous innovation, ensuring their relevance and impact in an ever-evolving landscape. Innovation is not a one-time achievement but an ongoing process. Influencers are encouraged to view challenges as opportunities, collaborate with diverse voices, communicate strategically, and redefine success beyond conventional metrics.

In this dynamic and interconnected digital age, innovation is not merely a choice; it is a necessity. Those influencers who dare to challenge norms, embrace adversity, and continuously evolve will undoubtedly shape the future of Christian influence, leaving a lasting impact on audiences around the world.[3]

5

FOUR COMPONENTS OF INFLUENCE

Repetition is a critical tool in any learning process. Vulnerability was addressed in chapter four, and it will be emphasized again in this chapter. That's just how important it is. But this time vulnerability will be joined by transparency, originality, and relatability as vital components for an effective Christian influencer. Quality lighting and fancy cameras are great to have, but they only enhance the experience. To have a memorable platform, you must focus on bringing your audience on a journey with you. Whether you are growing a business or expanding a ministry, you must pay attention to these four components.

VULNERABILITY: BUILDING TRUST THROUGH AUTHENTICITY

My journey started through my vulnerability on social media. Long before there was a Black Christian Influencers organization, there was an influencer by the name of Jackie the Educator. I created this platform in the hopes that I could relate to people better, and I often used vulnerability to bridge the gap. At church, testimony service is when you stand up and share what God has done in your life. While I was growing up, my mother would stand up to testify in church all the time. She would start off with, "I want to thank and praise God for being the author and the finisher of my faith," and end with, "When I think of the goodness of Jesus and all that he has done for me, my soul cries out 'Hallelujah!'" Somewhere in between she would share about her life—those moments when she felt like she was on the verge of giving up, but God intervened right in the nick of time. After she shared her testimony, people would often clap, dance, and shout, celebrating the goodness of God.

Being vulnerable about your life on social media can have the same effect. However, vulnerability on social media can be difficult because you don't get to audibly hear people's responses. What's more, it can be disheartening to share vulnerable aspects of your life and not get the response you were looking for. Unfortunately, social media is complicated in that you never quite know what people will think about what you share. In a church setting, you can judge the effectiveness of your testimony by claps and shouts from the congregation. But on social media, you have to use likes and comments. Though it takes some getting used to, they actually are more similar than they are different.

THE TRUST FACTOR: WHY VULNERABILITY MATTERS

Vulnerability isn't just about sharing—it's about building trust at scale. But in a digital space where success is often measured by likes, how do you know if your vulnerability is making an impact?

Here's a mindset shift:

Viral ≠ valuable. The most life-changing posts often don't go viral. Influence isn't just about reach; it's about depth.

Your real impact may be invisible. Some people will never like and comment on your posts or DM you, but your words may be exactly what they needed.

Are you leading or just exposing? Vulnerability should be about helping others, not just airing out pain for attention. Before you post, ask yourself, *Does this serve someone, or is it just for me?*

The true measure of influence through vulnerability isn't in public applause—it's in the silent lives being transformed behind the screen.

Sharing my testimony on social media was daunting, as it exposed a deeply vulnerable chapter of my life. After five years of marriage that many perceived as idyllic, I faced the unforeseen challenge of ending the relationship due to circumstances beyond my control. Despite my fears, opening up about this experience has profoundly impacted others. The outpouring of support and shared stories in response to my post underscores the power of vulnerability. One commenter expressed, "Your courage to share this gives me hope in my own journey." Another noted, "Thank you for your transparency; it's a reminder that we're not alone in our struggles." These heartfelt responses have reinforced my belief that by sharing our personal challenges, we can foster a sense of community and resilience among those facing similar trials.

TRANSPARENCY: FOSTERING CONNECTION THROUGH OPENNESS

Like vulnerability, transparency plays a significant role when it comes to connecting with others via social media. There are varying levels of transparency. You may assume it means being completely open about everything, but transparency on social media looks different for each person. You can be transparent without sharing every aspect of your life. For instance, some people post everything they eat, whether it's a slice of pizza or a cup of coffee from Starbucks. This level of transparency can sometimes be annoying and may not always be the best way to relate to your audience. Unfortunately, there are no classes that teach you how much is too much to share. But I will do my best to give you some examples to help you navigate these scenarios.

You must consider whether your transparency is relevant to your audience or just relevant to you. Oftentimes, we share because we are bored. That's not necessarily a bad thing, but sharing from a place of boredom can easily lead to sharing the wrong things. Boredom is an emotion, and sharing from an emotional state can cause you to lose sight of your true purpose. The thing that separates a regular person from an influencer is purpose. An influencer will likely have a target audience and a specific message that their audience comes to them to hear.

Most influencers are known for a specific niche. Having a niche will help you to focus your transparency. Instead of randomly sharing about every little thing that happens in your life, you can share about specific things as they relate to the niche you belong to. For instance, if I were a chef and my content was often about my journey as a chef, I would be less likely to talk about my wardrobe. As you develop as an influencer, you will learn to transition from one niche to another. But when you are first starting off, it's important to learn how to be focused in a specific area. Doing so will allow your audience to learn who you are and to trust your value. Later we will dive into the value of a niche, but for now, think about your specific area and how transparency can be targeted.

Being transparent with your audience means sharing the good, the bad, and the "I'd rather not talk about it" moments. We love to post our wins—the promotions, the glowing testimonials, the perfectly curated highlight reels. But when it comes to the messy middle, the setbacks, and the times we feel like throwing in the towel? Suddenly, we're on mute.

Life isn't just a collection of wins. Every great story, whether it's your favorite movie or a testimony that moves you, has conflict. The struggles make the victories meaningful. Would

AUTHENTICITY WINS. PEOPLE DON'T CONNECT WITH PERFECTION—THEY CONNECT WITH WHAT'S REAL.

you really root for a character in a movie who wins effortlessly the entire time? Probably not. You'd be asleep before the credits roll. The same goes for your audience. They need to see the full journey, not just the polished final product.

That's where safe levels of transparency come in—letting people in without letting it all hang out. For example, you can share how you battled self-doubt before launching your brand without diving into the deep end of your personal drama. Or you might talk about the financial struggles of building a business without dropping exact bank statements. It's about being real enough to be relatable but wise enough to keep some things private.

Learning this balance takes time, but you'll get the hang of it. Transparency isn't about turning your life into a reality show; it's about creating genuine connection while still maintaining some mystery. Let's be real: A little bit of mystery keeps people coming back for more.

ORIGINALITY: STANDING OUT WITH UNIQUE PERSPECTIVES

Being original is difficult when it comes to social media. People often utilize trends, and some become so lost in doing what others do that they lose sight of what sets them apart. Although it's important to use algorithms to gain visibility, it's also important that you have some originality in your platform that allows you to stand out.

Originality is a very important part of developing as an influencer. We are called to be set apart as Christian influencers, but the algorithm often makes it very difficult for us to find that distinction. However, understanding who our audience is will help us to focus on creating original content that stands out to those individuals. For instance, my company Black Christian Influencers has a platform that reaches a specific audience. The people who associate with this page often have nostalgic memories of Black culture and connect around experiences within the Black church. Keeping this in mind helps me to create original and relatable content.

Developing a unique voice and an original perspective is not an overnight process. It will require you to try many ways of communicating. You might think talking is the best method, but sometimes varying forms of communication are more effective. For instance, some people choose to dance, while others allow the written word to take the lead. Finding the best way to connect to your audience is the primary objective. Once you figure out a method that is well received, you can duplicate it and allow your voice to grow and deliver more messages. Many content creators have gone through trial and error before finding the method that works best for them.

Another important aspect of originality is creativity. These two go hand in hand in the process of developing content. Creativity and originality are necessary for capturing and keeping our audience's attention when we deliver a message. As we have learned in previous chapters, social media was designed for entertainment purposes. People later realized that it had the capacity to do so much more than entertain. However, this doesn't mean that its original purpose of entertaining should be forgotten. We must do our best to create content that not only informs our audience but also entices them to want to know more.

THE ORIGINALITY EQUATION: HOW TO STAND OUT IN A SATURATED SPACE

Social media rewards what's familiar, but real influence is built on what's distinct. In a world where everyone is recycling the same viral sounds, captions, and formats, how do you truly stand out?

The secret: Originality isn't just about creating—it's about courage.

If your content disappeared tomorrow, would anyone notice? Be honest. If the answer is no, your voice may be blending in too much.

Stop chasing visibility and start chasing impact. Being known isn't the same as being needed. What problem are you solving?

Your weird, niche perspective is your superpower. The more specific you are, the more people will connect with you. Generic gets ignored, while specific gets remembered.

It's easy to copy what's working for others, but true originality requires conviction. The question isn't "What's trending?" It's "What do I have to say that no one else can?"

Being creative is a necessity when attempting to grow as an influencer.

Innovation is another necessary component for originality. Most trends do not come from thin air. They often start from someone who had an innovative and original idea that caught on very quickly. Some of the most viral challenges on social media started with one person doing it and then other people following suit. For example, the Ice Bucket Challenge is one of those original and innovative ideas that caught on and, in a unique way, brought awareness to Amyotrophic Lateral Sclerosis (ALS), formerly known as Lou Gehrig's disease. The challenge was created by three individuals who wanted to draw awareness to the ALS community and increase donations to the cause. They did this by pouring ice-cold water over their heads and then challenging people to do the same. It caught on like wildfire, leading to more than seventeen million participants and raising $115 million for the ALS Association.[1]

RELATABILITY: CREATING CONNECTION WITH THE AUDIENCE

Being relatable is one of the most important factors in creating a connection with your audience. Influencers are unique because of their ability to relate to others. Movie stars, celebrities, and world-renowned recording artists gain their ticket to influence through exposure and notability. However, influencers gain prominence based on their ability to connect with their audiences. The significance of being relatable as an influencer is imperative to the craft.

Influencers grow because other people often see themselves in them. This aspect of connection creates a reality where the content creator feels less like a distant celebrity and more like a friend. This distinction is even reflected in the language used to describe their audiences: followers rather than fans.

Over time, the word *fan* has evolved. While it was once a widely accepted term for anyone who admired a public figure, it is now more commonly associated with individuals who have a strong, sometimes distant admiration for celebrities. In contrast, influencers foster a deeper connection with their audience, positioning them as like-minded supporters rather than distant admirers. This shift allows influencers to cultivate a community rather than just an audience.

Although the term *friend* is used loosely on social media, it has introduced new ways for influencers to engage with their audiences, creating tiered levels of connection. By fostering relatability, influencers break down the traditional barriers between public figures and their supporters, making their audience feel more personally invested in their journey.

Influencers are now able to interact with their audiences through comments and direct messaging, creating a sense of closeness that was once reserved for personal relationships. Receiving customized messages and responses from someone deemed influential helps followers feel more connected and valued. As you grow in your influence, it will become even more important to cultivate this sense of connection by encouraging your audience to not only remain fans but to grow as engaged followers and even as "friends." This level of interaction enhances their experience while deepening your impact as an influencer.

A strong parallel can be drawn between influencers and pastoral leadership. In many churches, members value the ability to reach their pastors and feel noticed and cared for. However, because a pastor cannot personally engage with every individual, churches often implement small groups led by trained leaders to foster closer relationships. Similarly, influencers must recognize the importance of setting boundaries while still maintaining a sense of accessibility.

Not every follower can have personal access, and it's essential to establish healthy limits to prevent burnout and maintain personal well-being. This might include setting designated times for engagement, using community moderators, or leveraging tools like newsletters and live Q&As to connect in a more structured way. The goal is to create meaningful relationships without overextending yourself, ensuring that your influence remains impactful, sustainable, and authentic.

ENHANCING INFLUENCE: BEYOND THE SURFACE LEVEL

As important as the elements previously described are for the advancement of your social media growth, you cannot ignore the importance of quality production. Everything from your lighting to your camera settings to your background ambience all contribute to your content growth.

Another component beyond the surface is your personal relationship with Christ. People often create content that has very little relevance to spiritual development, but this is a necessary component for believers to keep in mind as they create content. We are all called to be disciples of Christ and, whether we are entrepreneurs or life coaches, our goal should be to represent Christ well. So even if we are sharing something entertaining, we must remember that our content should not cross a line that would misrepresent the faith we uphold. We should always maintain a balance of creating content that captures attention without compromising our beliefs.

BRINGING IT ALL TOGETHER: NAVIGATING THE INFLUENCE JOURNEY

Learning to incorporate all the different components of vulnerability, transparency, originality, and relatability takes effort. It requires focusing less on trying to perfectly execute everything. Allowing yourself to lose control and follow your instincts around human interaction will be your best strategy.

When I became an influencer, I would often overthink what I should and shouldn't do. It became overwhelming to try to be perfect. What I found to be most helpful was following my instincts and allowing myself to learn from my mistakes. The process of making mistakes is what makes you even more authentic in your pursuit of becoming an influencer. Sometimes, simply sharing that you don't have all the answers is enough to gain your audience's trust. All the components mentioned in this chapter are strategies to do just that—gain trust. When you have the trust of your audience, you will be more at ease with showing your true self and focus less on being something that you are not. The goal of being an influencer is not to create an unsustainable narrative of yourself but to create the narrative of who you really are and share your consistent voice throughout your platform.

There are many ways for you to develop your skills as an influencer, but the most important one is to not become so focused on your own gain that you lose sight of what you are being called to do. Your assignment is not to edify your own profile but to help others through your own transparency. When you keep the attention on others and not on yourself, you stay focused on what really matters.

As you embark on your journey of growing as an influencer, I encourage you to continually ask yourself what the purpose of your platform is. This question will help you to consistently refocus on your goals and keep you from becoming self-serving in your agenda of being an influencer. It's easy to become narcissistic in your pursuit of growth, but remembering your purpose will allow you to recenter yourself on what matters most.

6

HOW TO GROW YOUR PLATFORM

Some people assume that growing a platform on social media is just about chasing clout or seeking validation. However, platform growth is necessary for expanding the message and vision God has given you. Without growth, the impact of social media is limited. One of its greatest benefits is the ability to share a single idea with thousands, even millions of people in seconds.

Imagine sharing your testimony in a room with ten people. The impact those ten people experience is powerful, but what if you could share that same testimony with *ten thousand* people? Social media makes that possible. Growing your platform isn't about fame—it's about reach. The more people who see your content, the greater your influence in spreading the message God has given you.

That said, growing an audience isn't easy. It requires strategy, consistency, and adaptability. The landscape of social media is always changing; what works today might not work tomorrow. By the time you read this, the algorithm may have shifted again. However, while specific growth tactics evolve, the core principles of platform growth remain the same.

So, if you're ready to grow your platform without losing yourself in the process, here are seven strategies to help you stand out and stay impactful.

DON'T LOSE YOURSELF TRYING TO GO VIRAL

Growing your platform is important, but not at the expense of your integrity. Though millions of people create content daily, not all content is valuable or meaningful. If you're not intentional about the why behind your content, it's easy to lose yourself in the process.

Some people start out with authenticity but end up chasing likes and validation. At first, it's just excitement from a viral post. But over time, that validation becomes addictive. Suddenly, they're no longer posting what they believe in but what they think will get attention. The message gets lost.

The validation-seeking nature of social media reminds me of high school. There's always pressure to fit in. When I was a freshman, a senior convinced me to ditch school and walk to his house. The entire time I felt uneasy, but I ignored my gut and went anyway. And once I got there, let's just say I almost made a decision I would have regretted for a very long time.

The same thing happens in content creation. If gaining followers requires you to compromise your values or step outside of your character, you've lost sight of your purpose. Chasing trends is one thing; sacrificing your authenticity is another. The key to lasting influence isn't just gaining an audience—it's doing so in a way that reflects who you truly are.

MAKE YOUR CONTENT SO GOOD PEOPLE HAVE TO SHARE IT

Shareable content is anything people find valuable enough to pass along. It's the digital version of word of mouth, allowing your message to spread far beyond your immediate audience. And the best part? It happens organically.

Shareable content doesn't have to be complicated. Sometimes, it's an encouraging message. Other times, it's a must-have product recommendation, a powerful sermon clip, or a choir breaking into a spontaneous praise break at a wedding. If people relate to it, they'll share it.

My grandmother had some of the best soul food recipes that became legendary among family and friends. Her pineapple cake was next level. Whenever she brought it to a gathering, people would line up for a slice, and before the night was over someone was asking for the recipe. I'd make the cake, and soon enough, people were asking me for the recipe. Before I knew it, my grandmother's cake was being enjoyed by folks she had never even met.

That's exactly how viral content works. When something is valuable, simple, and relatable, it spreads effortlessly.

YOUR NICHE IS YOUR SUPERPOWER—FIND IT AND OWN IT

I used to struggle with the word *niche*. It felt like a fancy way of saying, "Stick to one thing forever." But your niche is simply your way of strategically connecting with your audience.

Think of it like making a phone call. If you're trying to reach a friend, you don't just stand outside and yell their name, hoping they'll hear you. You pick up the phone, dial their number, and connect directly. Your niche is your phone line to the people you're called to serve.

Some people worry that choosing a niche means they'll be stuck in one lane forever. But that's not true. A niche is a starting point, not a prison. Your focus might start with business but later expand to faith-based leadership. You might begin as a music artist but eventually shift into mentoring others. The key is to give one area enough time to grow before jumping to the next.

Most of the time, your niche is tied to something people already come to you for. Ask your friends and family—what do they think you're naturally good at? Often, the things we struggle with the most become the areas we have the most wisdom in. Your pain points often lead you to your purpose.

STOP TRYING TO TALK TO EVERYONE— FOCUS ON WHO NEEDS YOU

Imagine you're at a party and you stand in the middle of the room yelling, "Hey, everybody! Listen to me!" Chances are that people will ignore you. But if you walk up to someone, introduce yourself, and start a meaningful conversation, they'll listen.

Social media works the same way.

Stop trying to reach everyone and focus on the right people.

The more specific your message, the more impact it will have.

A niche isn't limiting—it's clarifying. Who are you talking to, and why does your message matter to them?

YOU DON'T NEED TO BE LOUD, BUT YOU DO NEED TO BE SEEN

People scroll through social media quickly. If your content doesn't grab their attention in the first few seconds, they'll keep scrolling. An attention grabber is anything that makes someone stop and listen.

It could be a bold statement, a striking visual, or a compelling question. It could be something as simple as wearing a bright color or positioning yourself in an interesting location. The key difference between grabbing attention and seeking attention is purpose.

I once spoke at a high school event, and I knew that if I didn't keep their attention, I'd lose them within minutes. So I wore bright colors, smiled often, and intentionally engaged with students before I even got on stage. The way you present yourself plays a big role in how people receive your message, both online and in real life.

PAY ATTENTION TO WHO'S ENGAGING, NOT JUST WHO'S LIKING

Social media algorithms are not your enemy, but they do require strategy. Instead of obsessing over likes, pay attention to shares and comments.

If a post gets shared multiple times, that's a sign it's working. The algorithm prioritizes content that sparks engagement. If you notice a video performing well, create more content like it.

Also, don't be afraid to delete and rework content that isn't landing. I've posted things and taken them down within hours when I saw they weren't resonating. Trial and error is part of growth.

STOP OVERTHINKING AND JUST POST THE THING!

One of the biggest barriers to platform growth is overthinking.

I've met so many aspiring influencers who want every post to be perfect. They second-guess every caption, every angle, every edit. Meanwhile, someone else with half the talent is growing, simply because they're willing to post consistently.

Feedback is great, but don't become dependent on it. At some point, you have to trust yourself, trust your message, and just hit post.

While social media will keep evolving, the foundation of influence remains the same: Be valuable, be consistent, and be true to who God called you to be. Growth takes time, but if you're intentional, adaptable, and committed to your message, your platform will expand in ways you never imagined.

Now, go post that content. Your audience is waiting.

APPLYING WHAT YOU'VE LEARNED

Growing your platform isn't just about learning the right strategies—it's about actually putting them into action. To make sure you're applying what you've learned, use the checklist below to assess your progress. Then take it a step further by using the Content Planning Worksheet to start mapping out posts that align with your message and goals. The key to growth is knowing what to do and doing it consistently.

PLATFORM GROWTH CHECKLIST: ARE YOU ON THE RIGHT TRACK?

Use this checklist to evaluate how well you're applying the platform growth strategies. Be honest with yourself. This is a tool to help you improve!

Clarity and purpose—Am I clear on why I want to grow my platform?
- ☐ I know my mission and message.
- ☐ My content aligns with my values and doesn't compromise my integrity.
- ☐ I am not chasing trends at the expense of my authenticity.

Shareability—Is my content something people naturally want to share?
- ☐ I create posts that are valuable, relatable, or entertaining.
- ☐ My content solves a problem or encourages my audience.
- ☐ I am paying attention to which posts get shared and making more like them.

Niche and audience—Do I know who I'm talking to?
- ☐ I have identified my niche (faith-based leadership, business, lifestyle, etc.).

☐ My content is specific enough that people know what to expect from me.

☐ I am consistently creating content that serves my audience's needs.

Attention-grabbing—Am I causing people to stop scrolling?

☐ I use compelling visuals, headlines, or hooks at the start of my content.

☐ I consider how my appearance, setting, and energy affect engagement.

☐ I experiment with different styles of presenting my content.

Engagement and growth—Am I focusing on interaction, not just numbers?

☐ I engage with my audience by replying to comments, DMs, etc.

☐ I track shares and comments, not just likes.

☐ I am adjusting my content based on what resonates most with my audience.

Consistency and adaptability—Am I posting regularly and staying flexible?

☐ I have a posting schedule that keeps me active.

☐ I adapt my content based on feedback, trends, and platform changes.

☐ I don't let perfectionism stop me from posting!

YOUR SCORE	
18 checks	You're on fire! Keep refining and stay consistent.
12–17 checks	You're on the right track but have room for improvement.
6–11 checks	You're building momentum! Identify weak areas and make adjustments.
1–5 checks	Time to refocus! Start small and implement one strategy at a time.

Bonus

CONTENT PLANNING WORKSHEET

To make sure you're applying these strategies, Table 1 is a worksheet you can use to map out your content. This will help you track your progress and stay intentional about growing your platform. Remember, real growth happens through action. So check your boxes, plan your content, and start posting—your audience is waiting!

Table 1. Content Planning Worksheet

Post Type	Purpose (Encourage, Educate, Entertain)	Target Audience	Engagement Goal (Shares, Comments, Saves)	Posting Date
Example: Testimony about overcoming fear	Encourage	Young professionals	Comments and shares	Monday
Example: Quick tip for business owners	Educate	Christian entrepreneurs	Saves and shares	Wednesday
Example: Funny church meme	Entertain	General audience	Shares	Friday

7

NAVIGATING SOCIAL MEDIA

Keeping up with social media changes is like trying to catch the beat during a Sunday morning praise break, but you're that one offbeat Christian who just can't seem to get the rhythm right. While everyone else is clapping, stomping, and shouting on cue, you're in the corner jumping up and down, hoping for the best. Just when you think you've caught the groove, the tempo shifts, the organ modulates, and you're even more lost than before. Social media moves just as quickly. One minute you're finally getting comfortable with a platform, and the next, there's a new update, a new trend, or a whole new app. Suddenly, what worked yesterday is irrelevant today.

What's wild is how quickly social media has transformed from being simply a fun way to connect to a powerful tool for influence, business, and ministry. It wasn't always like this. Back in the early days, social media was a digital hangout spot. Myspace was one of the first places where we saw what an online community could look like. There was no pressure to build a brand or grow an audience. It was just a space to express yourself, show off your favorite music, and if you were feeling fancy, customize your page with glitter text and a background so bright it could give someone a headache. Nobody thought of Myspace as a business opportunity—it was just fun.

Then came Facebook, the platform that started as a college-only space before quickly turning into the digital family reunion where your aunt shares way too much. Twitter (now X) made its mark by giving people a space to share rapid-fire thoughts, break news, and—let's be real—argue. Instagram made us all believe we were professional photographers, Snapchat introduced disappearing messages and fun filters, and TikTok flipped everything upside down with short-form videos that could turn an everyday person into an overnight sensation. Just when we thought we had a handle on things, Clubhouse came through with live audio rooms, Periscope introduced live streaming, and Meta launched Threads to take on Twitter.

Social media has evolved so much that if you blink, you might miss the next big shift. To understand where we're headed, let's take a moment to reflect on where we've been. Each platform has introduced something new, shaping the way we share, connect, and influence. Table 2 is a snapshot of the major social media platforms and how they've changed the game.[1] Of course, by the time you read this, another platform will probably be making waves (or disappearing—RIP Vine).

Table 2. Major Social Media Platforms Chart

Platform	Launched	What Made It Unique?	Who Was Using It?
Myspace	2003	Customizable profiles, Top 8 friends, and autoplay music (which probably scared visitors)	Millennials and Gen X experimenting with online connection
Facebook	2004	Started as a college-only network, then became the digital family reunion where your aunt shares way too much	Millennials and Gen X young adults
Twitter (now X)	2006	Home of trending topics, breaking news, and the fastest way to get canceled	Journalists, influencers, thought leaders, and anyone with opinions
Instagram	2010	The app that made us believe we were all photographers and made filters a thing	Millennials, Gen Z, brands, and content creators
Snapchat	2011	Disappearing messages, funny filters, and the first real push into casual, "in-the-moment" content	Gen Z and younger millennials looking for quick, unfiltered conversations
Periscope	2015	Early livestreaming app that helped pave the way for Instagram Live and Facebook Live	Early adopters of video content and live engagement
TikTok	2016	Where viral trends are born and fifteen-second clips can make someone famous overnight	Gen Z, millennials, and anyone looking for entertainment
Clubhouse	2020	An audio-only platform where people gathered in rooms to have unfiltered, live conversations	Entrepreneurs, industry experts, and networking enthusiasts
Threads	2023	Meta's answer to Twitter, but with a friendlier vibe	People looking for real-time conversations without the chaos of Twitter/X

ARE YOU BUILDING A PLATFORM OR JUST BORROWING ONE?

Social media platforms are rented space; you don't own them. The algorithm can change, your account can get suspended, or a platform can fade into irrelevance overnight. If your entire brand is tied to one app, you're building on shaky ground.

Here's how to own your influence instead of just renting it:

Build an email list. Algorithms don't control emails—you do. A direct line to your audience ensures you can reach them no matter what happens online.

Create content that outlives trends. Viral moments fade, but timeless, valuable content keeps people coming back.

Diversify your presence. Don't put all your influence into one app. A website, podcast, or even in-person connections give your platform stability beyond social media.

Social media is a tool, not your foundation. Own your audience or risk losing them the moment a platform decides to move on without you.

While social media platforms change, the principle remains the same: People want to connect, be heard, and share their stories. Each of these platforms has introduced something new to how we engage online, but social media itself is here to stay. It has become as essential as the telephone or television—always evolving, always shifting, but never disappearing.

With that in mind, the real challenge isn't just keeping up but knowing how to navigate these spaces in a way that makes sense for you. Social media moves quickly, but that doesn't mean you need to be everywhere at once. The biggest mistake you can make is trying to jump on every new trend just to stay relevant. Instead of spreading yourself thin, focus on being intentional. Some people thrive on video-heavy platforms like TikTok, while others build deeper engagement through long-form content on YouTube or podcasting. The key isn't to master every platform but to stay adaptable, remain authentic, and use social media with purpose.

It's easy to get frustrated when platforms update their algorithms or when a new app suddenly becomes the talk of the town, but instead of resisting change, see it as an opportunity. The world will continue to evolve, and so should we. Whether you're still holding on to Facebook, thriving on TikTok, or cautiously exploring whatever new app is trending, the message remains the same: Embrace the evolution, stay flexible, and use these tools wisely.

Social media moves fast. One day a trend is everywhere, and the next, it's as forgotten as last year's New Year's resolutions. But while the landscape is always evolving, one thing remains the same: If you know how to use it strategically, social media can be one of your most powerful tools to amplify your message, expand your influence, and build meaningful connections.

For many people, especially those who don't love putting themselves out there, social media has made networking easier than ever. Instead of making awkward small talk at an event or trying to jump into a conversation at just the right moment, you can engage on your own terms. Susan Cain, author of *Quiet: The Power of Introverts in a World That Can't Stop Talking*, highlights that introverts excel in environments where they can think before responding rather than having to compete to be heard in a fast-paced discussion.[2] Social media offers a way to connect with depth, not just noise.

But as convenient as online networking is, let's be real: In-person connections still matter. And I get it—if the thought of walking up to strangers and introducing yourself makes you break out in a cold sweat, you're not alone. The good news? You don't have to work the room like an extrovert to make meaningful connections. Matthew Pollard, author of *The Introvert's Edge to Networking*, explains that introverts are great at networking when they focus on quality over quantity.[3] Instead of trying to talk to everyone in the room, focus on a few deeper conversations that truly lead somewhere.

If in-person networking still feels overwhelming, here are a few ways to make it more manageable:

- Be the one who listens more than talks. People love to feel heard, and you don't have to dominate a conversation to make an impact.

- Find a quiet moment to introduce yourself. You don't have to jump into an already loud conversation. Instead, catch someone one-on-one between sessions or near the refreshment table (pro tip: snacks make everything better).

- Follow up online. If talking to people in person feels overwhelming, use social media to build on that connection afterward. A simple "Great meeting you today!" message can go a long way.

- Give yourself permission to step away. Networking events don't have to drain you. Take breaks, breathe, and remember that you don't have to be on the whole time.

At the end of the day, social media is an incredible tool, but it's not a replacement for real-life relationships. It's a bridge that helps you to connect, engage, and start conversations that can later turn into real opportunities. So go ahead and use social media to network your way, but don't be afraid to show up in real life when it counts. If all else fails, just remember:

The mute button exists online, but in person you might just have to fake a phone call.

UNLOCKING YOUR FULL POTENTIAL: WHY YOU NEED MORE THAN JUST YOURSELF

As much as we'd all love to believe we can do everything on our own, the truth is, we'll never reach our highest potential without the right people in our corner. No matter how talented, driven, or resourceful we are, true success isn't a solo act—it's a collaborative effort. That's where social networking becomes a game-changing tool for anyone looking to grow their influence, expand their reach, and build meaningful connections.

One way I use social media strategically is to research people who can help me grow professionally and intentionally connect with them online, whether by sending a message, engaging with their content, or finding a way to add value to what they do. But my strategy doesn't stop there. When I know I'll be attending an event, I take the time to see who's going to be in the room before I get there. Doing so allows me to set up conversations before they even happen. Instead of struggling to break the ice, I walk in already knowing what topics I can bring up, what we might have in common, and how I can contribute to the discussion. That way, I'm not starting a conversation; I'm continuing it. This small shift removes the awkwardness of networking and makes every interaction feel more natural and intentional.

Social media has completely reshaped the way we communicate, build relationships, and even launch careers. More than just a tool for individual growth, it's also reshaping entire industries and redefining how businesses operate. Take my company, Black Christian Influencers, for example. The entire platform was built around leveraging social media to connect, inspire, and equip influencers. Why? In today's world, influencers are shaping consumer behavior more than traditional marketing ever could. Whether you're a business owner, a ministry leader, or someone trying to get their message heard, understanding the power of social media isn't optional— it's essential.

When I first launched BCI, I had zero business experience. But social media gave me the perfect space to test, learn, and adapt before ever turning my platform into a business. Before social media, people had to rely on expensive focus groups, surveys, and trial-and-error strategies just to understand what their audience needed. Now, all that information is just a poll, a question box, or a simple post away.

For example, when I was developing content for my conference, I didn't simply guess what people wanted to hear; I asked them directly. By using the Stories feature on Instagram, I surveyed my audience in real time and crafted sessions based on what they truly cared about. This kind of instant feedback is one of the most powerful (and underutilized) benefits of social media.

And that's just the beginning. If you're wondering how you can start using social media features to enhance your business or grow your brand, here are some simple, practical ways to leverage key tools on your platform:

- Instagram and Facebook Stories: Use the poll feature to get instant feedback on new ideas, ask questions to spark engagement, or use the quiz feature to educate your audience in a fun, interactive way. If you're launching a product or event, use the countdown sticker to build anticipation and remind your audience to stay tuned.

- Live video (Instagram Live, Facebook Live, YouTube Live, TikTok Live): Going live allows you to engage with your audience in real time. Whether you're doing a Q&A, sharing an update, or even hosting a virtual event, live videos create instant connection and increase visibility.

- DMs and personalized engagement: Don't underestimate the power of one-on-one connections. Sending a quick message to new followers, responding to comments with thoughtful replies, or even voice messaging in DMs can build deeper relationships and turn casual followers into loyal supporters.

- LinkedIn and Twitter (X) networking: Social media isn't just about growing your audience but also about growing your connections. LinkedIn is a great place to engage with professionals in your industry, while Twitter (X) allows for quick, real-time interactions with thought leaders, brands, and potential collaborators.

- User-generated content and testimonials: Want to build credibility? Encourage your audience to share their experiences with your brand by resharing their posts, featuring testimonials, or creating community challenges that showcase their involvement. These interactions not only increase engagement but also give social proof that strengthens your brand's reputation.

Social media is about strategically using the tools at your disposal to build engagement, gather insight, and create opportunities. It allows you to not only connect with your audience but also to learn from them, adjust to their needs, and build trust in ways that traditional marketing never could.

If you're serious about growing, stop trying to do everything alone. Social media has given us the ability to connect, research, and strategize like never before. Whether you're looking to build a brand, start a business, or simply expand your network, the opportunities are endless, but only if you're willing to use them.

NAVIGATING SOCIAL MEDIA RELATIONSHIPS: THE GOOD, THE BAD, AND THE PETTY

Social media has made communication easier in some ways and messier in others. It's allowed us to connect more quickly, reach farther, and engage more deeply, but it's also opened the door to misinterpretations, online arrogance, and the kind of digital drama that can ruin relationships before they even begin.

If you've ever been in any kind of relationship—romantic, professional, or with that one friend who always takes forever to text back—you know the struggles of verbal versus written communication. The absence of tone, facial expressions, and body language means that a simple comment can be misread, overanalyzed, and completely taken out of context. Add to that the fact that social media gives people a false sense of boldness, and you've got a recipe for disaster. Some folks will type things they would never say to someone's face just because they can.

This disassociation from real-world consequences has been wrecking friendships, relationships, and even business opportunities faster than ever. When things go wrong online, it can be harder to fix them because people often react emotionally before thinking things through. However, like any tool, social media is only as powerful as the person using it. Learning how to engage wisely and respond effectively is the key to navigating this space without damaging your witness, your relationships, or your brand.

HOW TO RESPOND TO NEGATIVE POSTS WITHOUT LOSING YOUR PEACE (OR YOUR PLATFORM)

It's bound to happen at some point—you say something online, and someone takes offense, misinterprets, or straight up comes for you. Whether it's an angry comment, a shady subtweet, or a full-blown call-out post, the way you respond can either build your credibility or damage your reputation.

Here's how to handle negativity on social media with wisdom and grace:

1. Pause before you post. Proverbs 15:1 says, "A gentle answer turns away wrath, but a harsh word stirs up anger." Before responding, take a moment to breathe, pray, and process. Reacting in anger rarely leads to a positive outcome. If needed, step away before engaging at all.

2. Decide if it's worth responding to. Not every comment needs a reply. Some people are just looking for an argument, and arguing with a fool only makes two fools. If it's clear that someone is intentionally being negative

or stirring the pot, ignore, mute, or block. Your peace is priceless.

3. Clarify before defending. If someone misunderstood your post, don't jump into defense mode. Instead, ask questions or restate your point calmly. For example, "I see how that could have been unclear. What I meant was . . ." This approach helps diffuse tension instead of escalating it.

4. Protect your influence, protect your integrity. Whether you're representing yourself, a business, or a ministry, your response is a reflection of your character. If Jesus had social media, do you think he'd be in the comments section arguing with strangers? Your words should align with your values, even when you're frustrated. The internet has a long memory, and something posted in frustration today can come back years later. Respond in a way that future you (and your audience) will be proud of.

5. Use humor and grace when possible. Sometimes a lighthearted or gracious response can de-escalate tension better than anything else. If someone is being overly critical, responding with kindness often catches them off guard. (But let's be real, this doesn't always work with internet trolls.)

6. When necessary, take it offline. If a serious misunderstanding happens, moving the conversation to a private message or a phone call can help avoid a public back-and-forth that benefits no one.

THE BIGGER PICTURE: HOW SOCIAL MEDIA IS RESHAPING RELATIONSHIPS

Social media hasn't just changed the way we communicate, but it's also changed the way we build relationships altogether. Once upon a time, people found friends, business partners, and even their spouses within their immediate community. Now, a few clicks, a hashtag search, and a well-crafted DM can connect you to like-minded individuals across the world.

This expansion of possibilities is incredible, but it also comes with its own set of challenges. Having too many choices can sometimes leave people paralyzed rather than committed, especially in romantic relationships.

Before social media, if someone was looking for a spouse, their options were mostly limited to their church, workplace, or social circles. Now, with dating apps, social media, and global connections, people are overwhelmed by the sheer number of options. Some people never settle down because they always think someone better is out there. Others get caught up in emotional affairs with people they've never even met in person.

It's the same with friendships and business relationships. Social media gives us access to thousands of potential connections, but true relationships require commitment, intentionality, and wisdom. Just because someone follows you, interacts with your content, or even collaborates with you doesn't mean they're meant to be part of your inner circle.

At the end of the day, social media is a powerful tool, but it requires intentionality. The way we communicate, respond to negativity, and build relationships online should reflect our values, wisdom, and integrity. It's easy to get caught up in digital drama, endless options, or reckless communication, but your words and actions online should ultimately align with who you are offline.

Choose wisely. Speak carefully. And remember, just because you can type it doesn't mean you should post it.

THE FILTERED REALITY: WHEN SOCIAL MEDIA DISTORTS THE TRUTH

Social media has reshaped our world in ways we never could have imagined. But beyond the exciting connections, business opportunities, and networking advantages, there are real conversations we need to have—conversations about privacy, mental health, and the way social media is quietly altering how we see ourselves and the world around us.

As someone who has long advocated for mental health awareness, I can't ignore how our obsession with social media is leading us into dangerous territory. We've become more self-absorbed, validation-seeking, and dare I say it, borderline narcissistic because of our dependence on likes, shares, and comments. Some people are so unhealthily attached to their online presence that they've created entire false realities— curated, filtered versions of themselves that barely resemble who they truly are.

THE MENTAL HEALTH CRISIS NO ONE IS TALKING ABOUT

The effects of filtered reality on mental health are alarming, and the research proves it. A study from the American Psychological Association found that excessive social media use is linked to higher levels of anxiety, depression, and body dissatisfaction.[4] It's not hard to see why. Social media bombards us with unrealistic expectations, convincing us that everyone else is thriving while we're struggling.

For children and teenagers, the effects are even more devastating. Young people are already navigating hormonal changes, social pressures, and self-identity struggles. Now, on top of that, they have to discern between reality and highly edited, AI-enhanced, perfectly curated versions of other people's lives. A report from the National Center for Health Statistics found that teenagers who spend more than four hours a day on social media are more likely to experience symptoms of depression and anxiety.[5]

Even as grown adults who have lived life, gained wisdom, and built confidence, we still struggle with separating reality from filtered reality. No matter how much we tell ourselves that "it's just social media," those carefully curated images, success stories, and highlight reels start to mess with our perception of what's real and what's manufactured.

THE RISE OF THE FILTERED SELF: WHEN REALITY GETS DISTORTED

We live in an era where filters do more than smooth out blemishes. They reshape faces, alter body proportions, and completely distort reality. With the rise of AI-driven technology, people are becoming masters at deception, presenting themselves in ways that aren't just slightly enhanced but completely fabricated.

The problem with filtered realities is that once you start believing in the version of yourself that only exists online, reality starts to feel like a letdown. It's like telling a lie. Repeat it long enough, and even you start to believe it.

But here's where it gets dangerous: When people spend so much time curating their digital identity, they start to lose their real one. That loss of authenticity is more than a minor inconvenience. It's a mental health crisis waiting to happen.

- Social comparison leads to insecurity. When all you see are perfectly curated lives, it's easy to feel like you're falling behind.

- Overexposure to unrealistic beauty standards fuels body dysmorphia. A study published in the National Library of Medicine found that social media exposure to edited images significantly increases body dissatisfaction, especially among young women.[6]

- An obsession with online validation can replace real-world fulfillment. The dopamine rush from likes and comments creates an addiction, but like any addiction, the high never lasts.

SO WHAT DO WE DO ABOUT IT?

It's not realistic to swear off social media completely (unless you plan on moving to the mountains and living off the grid, in which case, I respect that). But we can make intentional choices to use social media in a way that protects our mental health rather than destroys it.

Here are some ways to stay grounded in reality while still engaging online:

1. Limit your screen time. The more time you spend scrolling, the deeper the comparison trap. Set app limits or take regular social media breaks to remind yourself that life happens outside of your screen.

2. Unfollow unrealistic accounts. If someone's content makes you feel less than, insecure, or constantly in comparison mode, unfollow them. Your mental peace is more important than anyone's aesthetic feed.

3. Remind yourself that social media is a highlight reel. No one is posting their worst moments, struggles, or everyday realities. Keep that perspective in mind before you start feeling like everyone's life is better than yours.

4. Engage with authenticity. Instead of curating a perfect, unattainable version of yourself, commit to showing up as the real you. This doesn't mean oversharing, but it does mean choosing honesty over image.

5. Invest in real-life connections. Social media is a great tool, but it can't replace genuine, face-to-face relationships. Be intentional about spending time with people who know the real you, not just the online version of you.

Social media is a double-edged sword—it can either empower us or imprison us. The difference is how we choose to use it.

At the end of the day, you don't have to be a prisoner to perfection, a slave to validation, or a victim of comparison. You just have to be intentional, mindful, and willing to disconnect from the fake so you can reconnect with the real.

PROTECTING YOUR PRIVACY IN A WORLD THAT SHARES EVERYTHING

The beauty of social media is that it allows us to connect, inspire, and share our lives with people all over the world. The danger is that it also allows people we don't know—and don't want to know—to have access to our lives in ways we never intended. I learned this lesson the hard way.

When I first started as an influencer, I thought transparency was the key to authenticity. I posted everything: what I ate, where I was going, who I was with, and even where I planned to be next. It felt harmless at the time. After all, I was just sharing my life, right?

Wrong.

One day, I discovered I was being stalked by someone who had been tracking my movements through my social media posts. At first, it was unsettling. Then it became terrifying. This person had figured out where I worked, where I spent my free time, and even details about my family—all without ever having a conversation with me.

The moment that shook me the most was when I arrived at my job to find that the stalker had somehow gotten inside my office and left gifts for me. I had never met or spoken to this person. And yet, there were items he believed I needed, sitting on my desk.

It got worse.

A few weeks later, he showed up at my church and sent me a message during service. But this time it was about my children. He described exactly where my daughters were sitting and commented on how beautiful they were.

At that moment, my stomach dropped. This wasn't just about me anymore—it was about my family's safety.

I had to take immediate action, involving the authorities and threatening a restraining order to make it stop. But the damage had already been done. I had unknowingly given a total stranger the blueprint to my life, and it forced me to completely change the way I interacted online.

THE ILLUSION OF CONTROL: ONCE IT'S POSTED, IT'S PUBLIC

One of the biggest misconceptions about social media is the idea that we control our own narratives. We don't.

The moment you post something, it's no longer just yours. People can screenshot, share, misinterpret, or twist your words in ways you never intended. Even if you delete a post, there's no guarantee someone hasn't already saved it. And while most of us aren't thinking about worst-case scenarios when we share, there are people out there who don't have your best interests at heart.

That's why privacy isn't just a suggestion. It's a necessity.

HOW TO STAY AUTHENTIC WITHOUT SACRIFICING SAFETY

One of the reasons social media works is transparency. People connect with you when they feel like they know you. But being authentic doesn't mean being reckless. You can be open and real without putting yourself at risk. Here's how:

1. Use social media's built-in privacy features. Every major platform allows you to control who sees your content. Instagram, Facebook, and even Twitter (X) allow you to select specific audiences for each post. You can create Close Friends lists, limit post visibility, or even restrict certain followers from seeing certain content. Take advantage of these tools so not everything you share is for public consumption.

2. Wait before you post. Instead of posting your exact location in real time, wait until you've left the area before sharing. This approach prevents strangers from tracking your movements or showing up where you least expect them.

3. Be intentional about what you share. Just because something is exciting doesn't mean it needs to be public. If you're celebrating a new house, blur out the address before posting. If you're opening an important letter, make sure no personal information is visible. A few seconds of caution can save you from major regrets.

4. Listen to the people who love you. Sometimes we get so caught up in sharing that we don't see potential dangers. That's why it's important to have friends and family who can call us out when we're oversharing. I'll never forget the time I posted a letter I received in the mail and my sister pointed out that my address was clearly visible. I deleted it immediately, but that moment stuck with me. Don't get defensive when people try to protect you. They see things you might not.

5. Set boundaries on your engagement. Not everyone who follows you needs access to your life. If someone is making you uncomfortable, block them. If a conversation is heading in the wrong direction, mute it. Protecting your space is not being rude; it's being wise.

The internet never forgets. Every post, every comment, and every photo becomes part of your digital footprint. That doesn't mean you should live in fear, but it does mean you should live wisely.

Being an influencer, business owner, or simply an active social media user means learning the balance between authenticity and security. You can share your life without giving people the blueprint to your every move. You can be transparent without being an open target. And most importantly, you can be engaging without compromising your safety.

Ultimately, your platform means nothing if you're not here to use it.

FACT-CHECK: NOT EVERYTHING ON THE INTERNET IS GOSPEL

Ah, social media—the land of viral conspiracies, breaking "news," and that one friend who still thinks chain emails will bring them good luck if they forward them to ten people. If there's one thing social media has mastered, it's the ability to make anything sound like the truth, even when it's as made-up as your cousin's "I'm on my way" text when they haven't even left the house yet.

Once upon a time, misinformation was easier to spot. If a stranger on the street tried to convince you that Beyoncé secretly owns Mars, you'd probably laugh, walk away, and question their life choices. But online? If the font is professional enough and there's a "breaking news" banner, people will share it like it came straight from their favorite news outlet.

At one point, the term *alternative facts* was trending. It's a polite way to refer to bold-faced lies dressed up as truth. And let's be real: Alternative facts aren't just a political problem, they're a social media epidemic.

One of the biggest missteps we make online is assuming that someone knows what they're talking about just because they speak with authority. Passionate delivery doesn't equal accuracy. Some of the most shared "fact-based" posts online are nothing more than loud opinions in a fancy suit.

Consider this: You're scrolling through your feed, and you see a video of a guy with a microphone passionately declaring that eating three grapes a day will cure all diseases. He's intense. He's convincing. The comment section is full of "facts" and testimonials from people who "know someone" who tried it and was healed.

Before you know it, you're reconsidering your entire grocery list.

But wait, where's the research? Did a doctor say this, or is this just a guy who got a little too inspired watching a food documentary on Netflix?

This is how misinformation spreads—quickly, confidently, and without receipts.

One of the most dangerous things about social media is that information can be shared so many times that it feels true, even when it's completely false.

Let's do a quick exercise. How many times have you seen posts like these?

- "I heard Facebook is about to start charging ten dollars a month. Better share this or you'll get locked out!"
- "Breaking: [Insert celebrity name] just DIED in a tragic accident!" (Meanwhile, the celebrity is alive and well, sipping coffee somewhere.)
- "Doctors HATE her! This ONE trick will help you lose thirty pounds overnight!"

Sound familiar? These types of posts go viral constantly because people read, react, and reshare without ever verifying if they're true.

Social media is an opinion-heavy space. That's not always a bad thing, but if you're making major life decisions based on a Twitter thread or a TikTok rant, that's a problem.

HOW TO AVOID BEING THAT PERSON WHO SHARES FAKE NEWS

Want to make sure you're not contributing to the misinformation crisis? Here are some best practices to keep you on the right side of history:

1. Google it. If a post is making a shocking claim, take sixty seconds to do a quick Google search. If no reputable news source is reporting it, it's probably fake.

2. Check the source. If the website sounds sketchy (BreakingNews247.com or TheTruthYouNeverKnew.org), it's probably not legitimate. Stick to credible sources like Snopes, Reuters, AP News, or FactCheck.org.

3. Look for the date. Just because something is trending doesn't mean it's recent. A lot of people reshare old articles that have nothing to do with current events.

4. Be wary of screenshots. A screenshot of a headline is not proof. Anyone can Photoshop a fake tweet or an official-looking news headline. If you can't find a link to the article, don't believe it.

5. Recognize satire. There are actual satire sites (like *The Onion* and *Babylon Bee*) that post fake news for laughs. The problem is that some people don't realize it's satire. Before reacting, double-check the source to make sure

you're not getting worked up over something that was meant as a joke.

6. Pause before you share. If you can't verify it, don't spread it. If you still feel the need to share, at least add a disclaimer: "I haven't confirmed this, but I found it interesting." That way, you're not presenting it as fact.

HOW TO ENGAGE WITHOUT BEING THE MISINFORMATION POLICE

Nobody likes a self-appointed fact-checker who jumps into the comments with, "Actually, that's not true," on every single post. But you can still help people navigate what's real and what's not in a way that isn't obnoxious.

- Ask questions instead of attacking. Instead of, "You're wrong," try, "Where did you hear that? I'd love to read more about it."
- Drop the link and keep it moving. If you find a fact-checking article that debunks a claim, share it politely and leave it at that.
- Know when to let it go. Some people are committed to their version of reality, and no amount of fact-checking will change that. Sometimes, it's best to just disengage.

Social media is great for sharing, connecting, and engaging, but it's also a breeding ground for misinformation. If we're not careful, we can contribute to the problem instead of the solution. Remember: Just because it's viral doesn't mean it's valid. Before you hit that share button, take a second to pause, research, and think. Your reputation (and the internet) will thank you.

HOW TO MAKE SOCIAL MEDIA WORK FOR YOU
(AND NOT THE OTHER WAY AROUND)

Now that we've fully explored the dangers of social media, let's not act like it's all bad. Sure, it can be a toxic wasteland of misinformation, clout chasing, and people confidently being wrong in the comments, but it also comes with some serious benefits, especially when used with wisdom, strategy, and a little bit of common sense.

As someone who built an entire business online, I can confidently say that social media, when used with intention, is one of the most powerful tools you'll ever have access to (outside of the Holy Spirit, of course—let's not get crazy). It's not only about going viral or racking up followers but also about leveraging your platform to create real impact, open doors, and position yourself for opportunities you never saw coming.

One of the biggest mistakes people make on social media is thinking they need to be picture-perfect, ultra-polished, and always on-brand. But nobody connects with perfection. Think about the content that stops you mid-scroll. It's usually something real, relatable, or raw, not another perfectly staged "just woke up like this" selfie that took forty-seven attempts and a ring light.

If you want to grow a meaningful platform, don't just post for the sake of posting. Plant seeds.

- If you're a business owner, don't just post your product. Show why you created it, how it works, and what problem it solves.

- If you're a speaker, don't just post your sermon clip. Talk about what inspired your message and how you applied it to your own life.
- If you're a creative, don't just post your finished work. Share the process, the struggle, and the lessons you learned along the way.

People don't just want to see what you do. They want to know why you do it and how it can help them.

YOUR AUDIENCE IS BIGGER THAN YOU THINK (STOP PREACHING TO THE CHOIR)

A common mistake is thinking your only audience is the people who need what you offer. But your audience goes beyond customers, clients, and church members—it also includes people who do what you do, aspire to do what you do, or can help amplify what you do.

I once worked with a Christian therapist who was struggling to gain traction online. She was only speaking to potential clients, thereby ignoring a whole world of fellow therapists, ministry leaders, and mental health advocates who could learn from her, refer people to her, and even collaborate with her.

So we switched things up. Instead of just saying, "Here's why you should book a session," she started

- sharing insights for other therapists on faith-based counseling techniques.
- posting conversations for pastors about how to support mental health in their congregations.
- engaging in discussions about Christian wellness that positioned her as a thought leader, not just a service provider.

Your influence is about more than reaching customers. It's about building a network of people who can push your message further than you ever could alone.

At the end of the day, social media is a tool. And like any tool, it works best when you know how to use it. We've talked about the risks—the misinformation, the mental toll, the privacy concerns. But let's not forget the responsibility.

Your responsibility, in addition to being online, is to be intentional.

- Don't just post—plant. Give people something that lasts longer than a twenty-four-hour story.
- Don't just show up—engage. The best connections aren't built in the comments; they're built in conversations.
- Don't just count followers—build community. Influence isn't about numbers; it's about impact.

Social media can be a distraction, or it can be a divine tool. The difference is in how you use it.

8

MAKING DISCIPLES THROUGH INFLUENCE

As believers, we've been given a direct assignment: "Go and make disciples of all nations" (Matthew 28:19). But truthfully, many of us have kept our influence as local as our favorite coffee shop and as small as our group chat. For a long time, there were practical reasons for this. If you weren't a traveling evangelist or a missionary, your ability to reach people was limited to your physical location. That made sense . . . back then. But today, technology has changed the game. You can share a message from your living room and have it land in another country within minutes. The "all nations" Jesus spoke about? They're now just a click away.

Social media has removed the barriers that once kept our influence confined. We're no longer just called to serve the people in our pews—we're called to reach the people in our feeds.

I love talking about business strategies, platform growth, and maximizing digital influence, but influence without impact is empty. Beyond the brand deals, speaking engagements, and viral moments, our ultimate calling is to make disciples. Most people don't know that I'm an ordained minister. My father is a pastor, and I grew up understanding the power of both faith and technology. That's why I'm passionate about helping Christians navigate social media, not just as content creators but as digital evangelists.

In earlier chapters, we explored how stepping outside of your normal environment can unlock new opportunities. But now, let's take that a step further:

- What does it mean to use social media as a tool for discipleship?
- How do we ensure our platforms aren't just seen but are also making a difference?
- How can we create content that doesn't just go viral but transforms lives?

This chapter is about using your influence to build the kingdom. The future of discipleship isn't just happening inside church walls; it's happening in comment sections, DMs, and live streams that stretch across the world.

The key to success is not your aesthetic, not your follower count, not even your perfectly curated content—it's your story.

THE KEY TO SUCCESS ON SOCIAL MEDIA IS YOUR STORY.

It's what makes people lean in, listen, and ultimately connect. We live in a world that's oversaturated with voices, content, and opinions. Every day, thousands of posts fight for attention, but the ones that stand out are the ones that carry meaning. That's why storytelling is the most powerful tool you have, not just for branding or influence but for impact.

PAUL: A TESTIMONY WORTH TELLING

When I think about the greatest disciples in the Bible, I don't just think about their titles; I think about their transformation. And there's no greater example of transformation than Paul.

Before he became one of the most influential figures in Christian history, Paul was the last person you'd expect to be preaching the gospel. He was Saul of Tarsus, a man who spent his days hunting down Christians, dragging them out of their homes, and throwing them into prison. He made it his mission to destroy the church.

He was even there when Stephen, the first Christian martyr, was stoned to death. While others threw the rocks, Paul stood by, approving of what was happening. He was the very definition of an enemy of the gospel.

And yet, God had other plans.

After a dramatic encounter with Jesus on the road to Damascus, everything changed. The same man who once tried to silence believers became one of the loudest voices for the faith. He went from persecuting the church to planting churches, from tearing down the gospel to writing nearly one-third of the New Testament.

That's the power of a testimony. Paul's past didn't disqualify him; it made his story even more powerful. His transformation wasn't just about him—it was about what God could do through him.

And that same principle applies to you.

YOUR STORY CAN REACH BEYOND BORDERS

If Jesus physically walked into the room right now and asked you to share your story, what would you say? Would you confidently testify about how he's changed your life, or would you freeze, wondering if your journey is even worth telling?

Many people hesitate to share their testimony, not because they don't have one but because they don't think it's significant enough. They assume that only dramatic, movie script–worthy transformations are worth telling. But it's not about how big or small your story seems. It's about the fact that it's yours.

What makes a testimony powerful is the effect it has on others. When you share what God has done in your life, you're planting a seed. In a world where faith is often questioned and truth is constantly distorted, real testimonies stand out. That's why your message needs to have substance. People aren't looking for another motivational quote or another surface-level "blessing on blessings" post. They're looking for real stories—testimonies that show God's power at work in everyday lives.

This is why discipleship in the digital age requires more than just posting Scripture or sharing a sermon clip. It requires vulnerability, relatability, and a willingness to let people in.

CUT THROUGH THE NOISE: WHY AUTHENTICITY WINS

We live in an era when trust is hard to come by. Social media has created an environment where people doubt what they see, question what they hear, and second-guess everything. The polished personas, the staged authenticity, and the "let me share this struggle but only after I've already conquered it" approach have made people skeptical.

That's why real stories, not rehearsed ones, break through.

People don't just want to hear about your victories; they want to understand how you got there. The struggles, the setbacks, the doubts, the moments when you almost quit. That's what makes your testimony powerful.

Don't just share the highlight reel—share the full journey.

Don't be afraid to show the process before the outcome.

Don't let the pressure to "have it all together" rob you of the impact your story could have.

Jesus didn't recruit perfect people to spread the gospel. He called the broken, the flawed, and the ones society had counted out. And their testimonies changed the world.

HOW TO USE YOUR STORY FOR KINGDOM IMPACT

1. Highlight the before and after of your testimony. It doesn't have to be dramatic, but it does have to be meaningful. Ask yourself, *Where has God transformed me?*

2. Connect your story to a bigger purpose. Don't just share for the sake of sharing. Point people back to the One who made the transformation possible.

3. Meet people where they are. Speak in a way that makes your story accessible. You don't need a pulpit to disciple people. Sometimes you just need a post that meets them in their moment.

4. Keep it real. Perfection is forgettable. Honesty leaves a lasting impact.

Paul's story wasn't powerful because he was perfect—it was powerful because he *wasn't*. His testimony reached nations because people knew his past.

And your story? It has that same potential.

Don't underestimate how God can use your journey to encourage, disciple, and inspire others. In a world full of empty words, a testimony of real transformation will always stand out. So tell it.

Not because it makes you look good. But because it makes God look as powerful as he truly is.

THE POWER OF TWO-BY-TWO EVANGELISM

In 2020 the world experienced a massive shift, and for once, it wasn't because of a new iPhone release. The pandemic forced us into our homes, and the church had to face something it had been tiptoeing around for years: digital evangelism.

For the first time in centuries, ministry was no longer confined to a physical building. Sermons, Bible studies, and prayer meetings all had to go online. Churches that had been resistant to embracing digital spaces suddenly found themselves scrambling to figure out Zoom, Facebook Live, and YouTube streaming.

Granted, some ministries were already ahead of the curve. Transformation Church, led by Pastor Mike Todd, had been thriving in the digital space long before the pandemic hit. Their approach was about creating an entire online experience that engaged people beyond simply watching a sermon.

- They mastered short-form, high-impact content, making their messages go viral.
- They utilized YouTube, Instagram, and TikTok to keep conversations going throughout the week.
- They understood that church wasn't just a location but a community.

So when the world shut down, Transformation Church didn't miss a beat. Their content was already reaching millions before churches even realized they needed to pivot. The results spoke for themselves—their digital ministry exploded, reaching people who might have never stepped foot in a physical church.

Meanwhile, other churches had to play catch-up. I practically begged my father's church to embrace social media as a tool for ministry. We had conference calls, sure, but using social platforms to connect, disciple, and engage was still met with hesitation. Then, when the pandemic hit, there was no time to debate. You either adapted or became irrelevant.

But here's the real lesson: The church should never be playing catch-up when it comes to reaching people. We should already be ahead of the curve, using every tool available to spread the gospel.

And as we step into this new digital era, we also need to understand that we're not meant to do this alone.

THE POWER OF PARTNERSHIP: WHY JESUS NEVER SENT ANYONE ALONE

Jesus knew something about ministry that many of us still struggle with: We need each other.

When he sent out his disciples, he didn't tell them to go alone. Instead, he sent them out in pairs, two by two. And he told them, "The harvest is plentiful, but the workers are few. Ask the Lord of the harvest, therefore, to send out workers into his harvest field. Go! I am sending you out like lambs among wolves" (Luke 10:2-3).

From this passage, we learn two major things:

1. Jesus was intentional about partnership. He could have sent the disciples out individually. After all, wouldn't that

have covered more ground? But no, he knew that ministry is stronger when you have support.

2. Evangelism comes with challenges, and accountability matters. Jesus wasn't sending them into a comfortable situation. He literally called them "lambs among wolves." Knowing the journey wouldn't be easy, he made sure no one had to do it alone.

These same principles apply today.

Whether you're building a ministry, launching a business, creating content, or just trying to be a light in your workplace, having the right people around you is essential.

Even in the influencer space, the most successful creators aren't islands—they're part of a community. They collaborate, encourage one another, and keep each other accountable.

If you're a Christian influencer, you need other believers in your corner.

If you're a leader, you need people who sharpen you.

If you're a creative, you need people who challenge and inspire you.

Because isolation breeds discouragement.

And if Jesus—who could have done everything on his own—chose to build his ministry with a team, what makes us think we should go at it alone?

We live in a world where independence is celebrated, but isolation is dangerous. If the pandemic of 2020 taught us anything, it's that we're not designed to do life or ministry alone. The digital space has opened up endless opportunities for evangelism, but it has also increased the need for accountability, community, and real connection.

Jesus set the example. He sent his disciples out two by two for a reason. He knew they would need support, encouragement, and strength to stay focused on their mission.

So here's the real question: Who's walking this journey with you?

Because if you're trying to do it all alone, you're doing it wrong.

THE BURDEN OF INFLUENCE AND THE POWER OF ACCOUNTABILITY

Being an influencer or leader means showing up, even when you don't feel like it. I know this firsthand. There have been countless times when I've had to stand before a crowd, deliver an encouraging message, and pour into others all while privately wrestling with my own faith, doubts, and struggles. If you've been in this position, you know how exhausting it can be. People expect you to have all the answers, but what happens when you have more questions than answers yourself?

Unfortunately, this isn't talked about nearly enough. There's an unspoken pressure to always be "on," to always have a word of encouragement, and to never let them see you sweat. But the truth is, being a leader doesn't make you immune to doubt, pain, frustration, or exhaustion. Even the most anointed, faith-filled leaders have moments when they question everything.

That's not new. If you need proof, just open the Psalms, a book filled with the rawest emotions of worshippers who both praised God and wrestled with their deepest pains. One moment David is declaring the Lord is his shepherd, and the next he's crying out, "How long, LORD? Will you forget me forever?" (Psalm 13:1). Sound familiar? Faith isn't the absence of struggle—it's trusting God through it.

But here's where things get tricky for influencers: When your brand is built on faith, who do you turn to when your own faith feels shaky?

THE POWER OF HONEST ACCOUNTABILITY

One of the best things you can do as a leader is to prioritize accountability. I always tell my influential friends to find at least one person they can be completely honest with about their struggles. Carrying everything alone is a setup for burnout and spiritual exhaustion.

For me, that person is my younger sister.

Since the very beginning of my journey as an influencer, she's been my right hand, my assistant, my business partner, and let's be honest, my occasional unpaid therapist.

If you've ever watched *Frozen*, you know exactly what I mean when I say I'm Elsa and she's my Anna. You know, the younger sister who refuses to let her older sister spiral alone, who follows her into the unknown (literally), and who constantly reminds her that she doesn't have to carry the weight of the world by herself? That's my sister.

Like Anna, she has made it her personal mission to make sure I don't isolate myself, overwork myself, or let the pressure of influence consume me. If I'm slipping in any area—whether it's my faith, my health, or my mindset—she's the first one to step in, and she does it with love . . . and just enough side-eye to let me know she means business.

Elsa needed that. If it weren't for Anna's persistence, Elsa would have stayed locked away in her ice castle, convinced she had to bear the burden alone. Meanwhile, Anna was climbing mountains, battling wolves, and tracking down her sister in subzero temperatures all because she refused to let her go through it alone.

If that's not a model of biblical accountability, I don't know what is.

The truth is, accountability isn't always fun. Sometimes I don't want to hear that I need to slow down, refocus, or take a step back. But when you have people in your life who are assigned to walk with you, they don't let you go too far without bringing you back. That's exactly why Jesus sent his disciples out two by two. He knew the road would be hard. He knew discouragement, exhaustion, and doubt would come. And he knew that having the right person beside you makes all the difference.

THE TAKEAWAY: FIND YOUR ANNA, OR BE ONE TO SOMEONE ELSE

Every leader, influencer, and believer needs an Anna. Someone who refuses to let them walk through the hard seasons alone. Someone who will check on them, call them out (in love), and remind them that they don't have to carry everything by themselves.

If you don't have an Anna in your life yet, maybe you need to be one for someone else. Real discipleship isn't just about leading—it's about walking with people, holding them up when they're weak, and refusing to let them do life alone.

You don't have to be the loudest, the strongest, or the most experienced person in the room. You just have to be willing to show up, stand beside someone, and remind them that they are not in this alone. If that means fighting through the metaphorical snowstorm to bring them back, then lace up your boots, because that's what accountability looks like.

Oh, and if you happen to break into a spontaneous duet along the way? That's just a bonus.

BECOMING BETTER SOWERS

If there's one thing Jesus made clear in Luke 10, it's that the harvest is plentiful, meaning there are countless people in need of the gospel. This is even more relevant today. But we must recognize that harvesting is work. Anyone who has ever planted anything, from a small backyard garden to an entire farm, knows that you don't just scatter seeds and hope for the best. There's a process. There's strategy. And most importantly, there are tools that make harvesting more efficient.

In the early days of farming, everything had to be done by hand. Crops were harvested one at a time, an exhausting and slow process. But as technology advanced, so did farming techniques. Now, entire fields can be harvested in hours rather than weeks, all because farmers embraced the right tools. Yet when it comes to evangelism, so many of us are still doing things the old way. We're planting seeds one by one, refusing to embrace the tools that could help us reach more people. Why struggle to plant one seed at a time when God has given us platforms that can reach thousands in a single moment?

Social media, digital platforms, and networking tools aren't just distractions—they are today's harvesting equipment. When used intentionally, they allow us to share the gospel at a scale that was once impossible. Jesus didn't overcomplicate his teachings. He used parables, stories, and simple truths to reach people where they were. If he were walking the earth today, you better believe he'd be using every tool available to reach the masses.

But even as we embrace the power of reaching people in large numbers, we must never forget the value of one-on-one interactions.

THE VALUE OF PLANTING SEEDS ONE AT A TIME

While large-scale evangelism is an incredible opportunity, there is still something deeply powerful about planting seeds individually, with care and intention. There's a reason why Jesus didn't just preach to crowds; he also met with people one-on-one. He had intimate conversations with individuals like Nicodemus, the Samaritan woman at the well, and Zacchaeus. He saw people, engaged them personally, and met them where they were.

Yes, reaching the masses is important, but discipleship doesn't stop at exposure. It thrives in relationship. Sometimes, the most transformative moments happen not in a viral post or a large sermon but in a direct message, a one-on-one conversation, or a personal follow up.

A farmer can scatter seeds across an entire field, but some seeds require careful planting, watering, and tending. Some hearts aren't won through broad messages; they need personal investment, patience, and intentional care.

Social media can introduce people to the message of Christ, but discipleship often happens in the follow up. When someone engages with your content, asks a deeper question, or shares a personal struggle, that's a chance to shift from broadcasting the message to cultivating it in an individual's life. We must be intentional about balancing both methods. Embrace the ability to reach many, but don't neglect the power of reaching one.

MAKING THE GOSPEL ACCESSIBLE: SIMPLICITY IS KEY

One of the biggest mistakes we can make as believers is over-complicating the gospel. The message of Jesus was never meant to be buried under theological jargon or presented in a way that makes people feel like they need a seminary degree to understand it. As a former educator, I learned firsthand that clarity is everything. The best teachers understand that if you want people to grasp what you're saying, you have to communicate in a way that meets them at their level. That's why most literacy experts agree that writing at a sixth-grade reading level is the most effective way to reach broad audiences.[1]

Before anyone thinks that's dumbing things down, let me remind you: Jesus didn't teach with lofty, academic language; rather, he used simple, relatable stories. He talked about farmers, fishermen, lost sheep, and mustard seeds—things people could visualize and connect with. That was intentional. This approach isn't just about making things "easier" for people. It's about making sure the message is received. A staggering 54 percent of adults in the United States (ages sixteen to seventy-four) read below a sixth-grade level, meaning that if we want to be effective disciple makers, we need to communicate in ways that ensure people understand and absorb the message.[2] However, clarity isn't just about words; it's also about how we engage. On social media, it's easy to dismiss people's questions, ignore criticism, or get frustrated when someone asks something that seems obvious. But discipleship requires patience and a willingness to explain, to repeat, and to meet people where they are, even when it's inconvenient.

As Christian influencers, our goal shouldn't be to sound impressive. It should be to make Jesus known.

DIFFERENT STYLES FOR DIFFERENT PEOPLE: EMBRACING DIVERSITY IN DISCIPLESHIP

There's no one-size-fits-all approach to evangelism. If there were, Jesus would have picked twelve identical disciples instead of a group that ranged from fishermen to tax collectors to a guy known for doubting everything. Discipleship is not about making everyone the same—it's about reaching people in different ways. Some people connect with deep theological discussions, while others need practical, relatable applications. Some prefer intellectual reasoning, while others are drawn in by passionate, emotional testimonies.

For example, I love engaging with people who are both intellectual and hopeful, who blend logic with faith and optimism. My older sister, on the other hand, is a professor who thrives on structure and rational discourse. Her approach is more methodical, analytical, and balanced, and she prefers teachers who break things down with careful reasoning and step-by-step clarity. Neither of us is wrong. We just connect with different approaches. That's why it's so important to embrace the differences in discipleship styles. Just like there are different learning styles (visual, auditory, kinesthetic), there are also different teaching styles that resonate with different people. The goal isn't to fit everyone into one mold but to make sure everyone has access to the message in a way they can receive it.

For those who want to dig deeper into learning and teaching styles, there are incredible resources available. Books like *Teaching to Change Lives* by Howard Hendricks and *The Art of Teaching* by Gilbert Highet provide practical insights on how to make the gospel clear, engaging, and transformative. The harvest is plentiful, but if we're going to be effective sowers, we have to use the right tools. We have to embrace new methods while staying faithful to the message. We have to simplify our approach without losing depth. And most importantly, we have to recognize that different people connect with different styles, so we need all kinds of disciples to reach all kinds of people.

If Jesus handpicked a diverse group of disciples to spread his message, then maybe we should stop trying to fit evangelism into one particular style and start embracing the differences that make us stronger. At the end of the day, the goal isn't just to scatter seeds—it's to bring in the harvest. And if we're serious about making disciples through influence, it's time to sow smarter.

9

STEWARDING YOUR INFLUENCE WELL

If you've made it this far, congratulations! You are officially in the influencer discipleship masterclass. Okay, maybe not officially, but at this point you should have a strong grasp of what it takes to use your platform for kingdom impact. Before you log off and start crafting your next viral post, we have to talk about stewardship, because how you handle your influence matters just as much as having it. Influence is a gift. It's also a responsibility. And if we're not intentional, we can easily get caught up in distractions, temptations, and the pressure to conform to what's trending instead of what's true.

Stewardship is about managing well what you've been given. It's a biblical principle that applies to every area of life—your finances, your time, your relationships, and yes, even your influence. Your platform, no matter how big or small, is something you've been entrusted with. The question is, are you using it wisely?

OBSTACLES TO INFLUENCE: THE FILTERS, THE FEARS, AND THE LIES

If you've spent any time on social media, you already know it's the land of highlight reels and curated personas. People post the best, most polished versions of themselves while cropping out the struggle, the failures, and the unflattering angles. While there's nothing wrong with curating your content, the problem comes when comparison sneaks in and starts distorting reality.

Social media has taken the age-old struggle of keeping up with the Joneses and put it on steroids. Instead of just envying our next-door neighbor's new car, we're comparing our lives to influencers who seem to have the perfect family, the perfect business, and the perfect faith journey all wrapped up in aesthetically pleasing content that makes us feel like we're somehow falling behind. But here's the truth: Comparison is a thief, and social media just gives it more doors to break into. The issue goes beyond the comparisons; it's that many of us are measuring ourselves against something that isn't even real.

There are people who edit their faces and bodies beyond recognition, curate their lives in ways that make them look more successful than they are, and only post the highs while con-

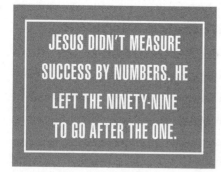

JESUS DIDN'T MEASURE SUCCESS BY NUMBERS. HE LEFT THE NINETY-NINE TO GO AFTER THE ONE.

cealing the lows. Without realizing it, we begin to measure our unfiltered lives against someone else's filtered reality.

Even worse, we start to believe that our impact is determined by numbers. That if we don't have thousands of followers, our voice isn't important. That if our content doesn't go viral, our message doesn't matter.

And that's a lie.

Jesus didn't seek crowds—crowds sought him. His impact wasn't in viral moments but in deep, transformative encounters that changed people's lives. Your worth isn't tied to your following. Your message isn't less valuable because it doesn't reach millions. If you impact one person, you've made a difference.

THE FEAR OF MISUSING INFLUENCE

Many Christian influencers wrestle with the tension between boldness and humility. You want to share your message, but you don't want to seem self-promoting. You want to be authentic, but you don't want to overshare. You want to inspire people, but you don't want to be seen as performative. Let's clear this up: Influence is not the enemy. Idolatry is.

The problem isn't that you have a platform; it's if you make your platform an idol. If your goal shifts from serving to self-promotion, that's where the issue lies. On the other hand, being hesitant to use the platform God has given you out of fear of seeming prideful is just as dangerous as being reckless with it. Look at Moses. When God called him to lead, he kept saying, "Who am I that I should go . . . ?" (Exodus 3:11). He doubted his abilities, his voice, and his worthiness to carry the message. But God wasn't asking for perfection. He was asking for obedience. Your job is not to shrink back out of fear but to show up in obedience.

If you ever wonder whether you're crossing the line into self-glorification, here's a simple check:

- Are you pointing people toward Jesus or toward yourself?
- Are you chasing influence for validation or using it for impact?

- Are you more concerned with numbers than with serving well?

The moment your platform becomes about building your name instead of his, you've lost your way.

PRACTICAL STRATEGIES FOR STEWARDING YOUR INFLUENCE WELL

1. Prioritize depth over reach. One engaged, transformed life is worth more than ten thousand passive likes. Don't fall into the trap of chasing numbers over nurturing relationships. Jesus impacted people deeply *and* widely.

2. Set boundaries for your mental and spiritual health. Like any tool, social media can harm you if you use it without restraint. Set time limits for scrolling, unfollow accounts that trigger comparison or distraction, and take social media breaks when needed. Your soul matters more than your stats. Protect it.

3. Don't let engagement define your worth. Your value is not measured in likes, comments, or shares. If Jesus based his success on public approval, his ministry would have ended the moment people turned against him. Your obedience is the goal, not applause.

4. Find a community of accountability. Influence should never be stewarded alone. Surround yourself with trusted friends or mentors who will challenge you, correct you, and support you.

FINISHING STRONG: STEWARDING YOUR INFLUENCE FOR THE LONG HAUL

Stewarding your influence well isn't about being perfect; it's about staying committed to the mission even when it's hard. The greatest influencers in the Bible—Paul, Peter, Moses— were not perfect. They messed up. They doubted. They had moments of weakness. But what set them apart was their willingness to keep going. As you step forward into whatever God has called you to do, remember this: You don't have to be the loudest voice in the room. You just have to be a faithful one.

Now, go steward your influence well.

ACKNOWLEDGMENTS

No journey is walked alone, and I am deeply grateful for the many people who have influenced, encouraged, and poured into me along the way.

To my parents, Tanya and Michael Horbrook, your faith, wisdom, and unwavering love have shaped me more than words can express. Thank you for your prayers, sacrifices, and example.

To my pastors, Pastor John Hannah and Pastor Glenn, your leadership and teaching have profoundly impacted my life. Thank you for guiding me in faith and purpose.

To my Aunt Jackie, your strength and wisdom have inspired me in countless ways. Thank you for always pushing me to be my best.

To my siblings and my family, your love and support mean everything. Thank you for cheering me on and reminding me of who I am.

And to every influencer who has helped shape my journey, whether in my life or from afar, knowingly or unknowingly: Thank you. Your impact is a reminder that influence is never just about us but about the lives we touch and the legacy we leave.

With gratitude,

Jackie the Educator

SUGGESTED RESOURCES

As you embark on your own journey of influence, I want to equip you with tools, books, and resources that will help you grow spiritually, strategically, and practically. These recommendations will support you in strengthening your faith, refining your message, and maximizing your impact.

BOOKS ON FAITH AND INFLUENCE

- *The Purpose Driven Life*—Rick Warren
- *Crushing: God Turns Pressure into Power*—T. D. Jakes
- *The Blessed Life*—Robert Morris
- *Discerning the Voice of God*—Priscilla Shirer
- *Spiritual Leadership*—J. Oswald Sanders

BOOKS ON LEADERSHIP AND IMPACT

- *Leaders Eat Last*—Simon Sinek
- *The 21 Irrefutable Laws of Leadership*—John C. Maxwell
- *Atomic Habits*—James Clear
- *Start with Why*—Simon Sinek
- *Dare to Lead*—Brené Brown

RESOURCES FOR CHRISTIAN INFLUENCERS AND CONTENT CREATORS

- YouVersion Bible App—daily devotionals and reading plans to keep you spiritually grounded
- Canva—a simple, free tool for creating professional graphics for social media
- Buffer or Hootsuite—scheduling tools to help you manage your social media effectively
- Unsplash or Pexels—free high-quality images for your digital content
- Anchor by Spotify—a free platform for launching your own podcast

COMMUNITIES AND CONFERENCES FOR CHRISTIAN LEADERS AND INFLUENCERS

- Black Christian Influencers (BCI)—a network for Christian content creators, speakers, and leaders
- Influence Network—a community of faith-driven entrepreneurs and influencers
- Christian Leadership Alliance—resources and training for Christian leaders
- Social Media Marketing World—a conference for growing and leveraging your platform

BIBLE VERSES ON INFLUENCE AND PURPOSE

- Matthew 5:14 (ESV): "You are the light of the world. A city set on a hill cannot be hidden."
- Proverbs 11:25: "A generous person will prosper; whoever refreshes others will be refreshed."

- 2 Corinthians 5:20: "We are therefore Christ's ambassadors, as though God were making his appeal through us."
- Colossians 3:23: "Whatever you do, work at it with all your heart, as working for the Lord, not for human masters."

I pray these resources equip and encourage you as you step boldly into your calling. Keep learning, keep growing, and most importantly, keep making an impact that points back to Christ!

NOTES

1. THE CALL TO INFLUENCE

[1] Brooke Auxier and Monica Anderson, "Social Media Use in 2021," Pew Research, April 7, 2021, www.pewresearch.org/internet/2021/04/07/social-media-use-in-2021/.

[2] Ani Petrosyan, "Number of Internet and Social Media Users Worldwide as of February 2025," Statista, April 1, 2025, www.statista.com/statistics/617136/digital-population-worldwide/.

[3] Pew Research Center, "Religious 'Nones' in America: Who They Are and What They Believe," January 24, 2024, www.pewresearch.org/religion/2024/01/24/religious-nones-in-america-who-they-are-and-what-they-believe/.

3. MARKETING AND EXCELLENCE MATTER

[1] For more details on SMART goals, see G. T. Doran, "There's a S.M.A.R.T. Way to Write Management's Goals and Objectives," *Management Review*, no. 70 (1981): 35-36.

4. INNOVATION REQUIRED

[1] R. Keith Sawyer, *Group Genius: The Creative Power of Collaboration* (Basic Books, 2007).

[2] Henry Jenkins, *Convergence Culture: Where Old and New Media Collide* (New York University Press, 2006).

[3] Phil Cooke, *Unique: Telling Your Story in the Age of Brands and Social Media* (Greenleaf Book Group Press, 2012).

5. FOUR COMPONENTS OF INFLUENCE

[1] "The ALS Ice Bucket Challenge: 10th Anniversary," The ALS Association, accessed February 15, 2025, www.als.org/ibc.

7. NAVIGATING SOCIAL MEDIA

[1] Samantha Lile, "Complete History of Social Media: Then and Now," Small Business Trends, December 17, 2024, https://smallbiztrends.com/2013/05/the-complete-history-of-social-media-infographic.html.

[2] Susan Cain, *Quiet: The Power of Introverts in a World That Can't Stop Talking* (Crown, 2013).

[3] Matthew Pollard, *The Introvert's Edge to Networking* (HarperCollins Leadership, 2021).

[4] Kirsten Weir, "Social Media Brings Benefits and Risks to Teens," *American Psychological Association* 54, no. 6 (September 1, 2023), www.apa.org/monitor/2023/09/protecting-teens-on-social-media#:~:text=A%20large%20body%20of%20research,depressive%20symptoms%2C%20especially%20among%20girls.

[5] "Daily Screen Time Among Teenagers: United States, July 2021-December 2023," NCHS Data Brief No. 513, October 2024, CDC, National Center for Health Statistics, www.cdc.gov/nchs/products/databriefs/db513.htm#:~:text=Teenagers%20who%20had%204%20or,daily%20screen%20time%20(9.5%25).

[6] "Instagram Use and Body Dissatisfaction," National Library of Medicine, January 29, 2022, https://pmc.ncbi.nlm.nih.gov/articles/PMC8834897/#:~:text=The%20first%20study%20in%20this,comparison%20with%20social%20media%20influencers.

8. MAKING DISCIPLES THROUGH INFLUENCE

[1] "Extending the Reach of Science—Talk in Plain Language," National Library of Medicine, October 25, 2021, https://pmc.ncbi.nlm.nih.gov/articles/PMC8591452/.

[2] "U.S. State and County Estimates Resources," National Center for Education Statistics, Program for the International Assessment of Adult Competencies, accessed July 2, 2025, https://nces.ed.gov/surveys/piaac/state-county-estimates.asp#4.

ABOUT THE AUTHOR

Jacqulyne Horbrook, also recognized as "Jackie the Educator" across social media platforms, hails from Chicago, emerging as a pioneering force among millennials. Armed with a master's degree in education and a bachelor's degree in business, her vision is to be renowned as a kingdom solutionist.

She serves as the visionary CEO of Black Christian Influencers (BCI), a thriving community dedicated to empowering kingdom builders across diverse professions. Additionally, she presides over two other flourishing enterprises: BCI Influencer Agency and the Christian Travel Club.

Ordained as a minister, her unwavering commitment lies in advancing the kingdom of God, leveraging her manifold talents and gifts.

Instagram: jackietheeducator
jackietheeducator.com

Like this book?

Scan the code to discover more content like this!

Get on IVP's email list to receive special offers, exclusive book news, and thoughtful content from your favorite authors on topics you care about.

 InterVarsity Press